Al Capp

Li'l ABNER®

THE FRAZETTA YEARS

VOLUME 2 1956-1957

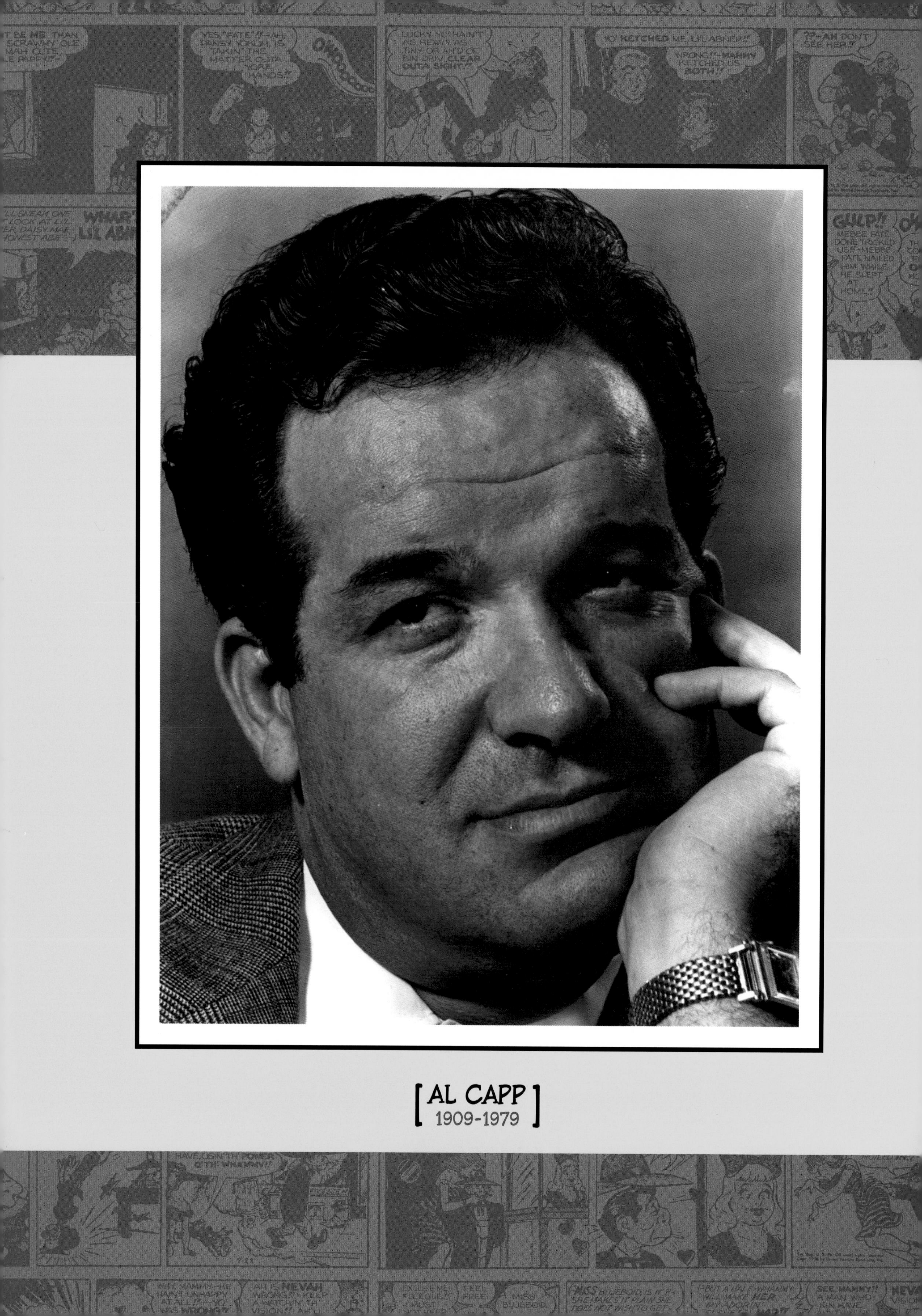

[AL CAPP
1909-1979]

Al Capp

Li'l ABNER®

THE FRAZETTA YEARS

VOLUME 2 1956-1957

EDITED AND COMMENTARY BY

Denis Kitchen

DARK HORSE COMICS®

CONTRIBUTING ARTISTS
Andy Amato, Harvey Curtis, Frank Frazetta, and Walter Johnson

DARK HORSE EDITORS
Dave Land and Philip W. Simon

ART DIRECTOR
Mark Cox

DESIGNER
Lia Ribacchi

PUBLISHER
Mike Richardson

AL CAPP'S LI'L ABNER: THE FRAZETTA YEARS VOLUME 2

Dark Horse Comics, Inc.,
10956 SE Main Street, Milwaukie, OR 97222

www.darkhorse.com

Sunday comic pages reproduced in this volume are from the collections of Bill Blackbeard and Denis Kitchen. Original artwork used in this volume came from the collections of Denis Kitchen and Joe & Nadia Mannarino (All-Star Auctions).

For more information about Li'l Abner, visit the official web site of Capp Enterprises, Inc. at www.lil-abner.com.

For out-of-print Li'l Abner books and related Al Capp memorabilia visit Steve Krupp's Gallery & Curio Shoppe at www.deniskitchen.com.

If you have an interest in licensing Li'l Abner, Shmoo, Fearless Fosdick, or related Dogpatch characters for merchandise, contact Denis Kitchen Art Agency, the licensing agent for Capp Enterprises, Inc., at agency@deniskitchen.com.

The editor of this series seeks old newspaper clippings, magazine articles, trade magazine ads, correspondence, memorabilia, artwork, and certain licensed merchandise related to Al Capp and the world of Li'l Abner. In addition, if you own original "Li'l Abner" artwork that you would allow to be scanned for future volumes of this series, please contact us as well. E-mail denis@deniskitchen.com or write: DKAA, P.O. Box 9514, North Amherst, MA 01054-9514.

Comic Shop Locator Service: (888) 266-4226

First edition: October 2003
ISBN: 1-56971-976-4

1 3 5 7 9 10 8 6 4 2

PRINTED IN CHINA

18 COMICS — Sunday Mirror — 15¢

NEW YORK, N. Y.   SUNDAY, NOVEMBER 27, 1955

LI'L ABNER by Al Capp

I JUST FLEW IN FROM EUROPE, TO SEE BIG JULIUS!! - GOTTA LEAVE IN 10 MINUTES!!

BIG JULIUS SPECIALLY SENT FOR ME, FROM HOLLYWOOD!! - HE NEEDS ME.!!

IF I DON'T GET BIG JULIUS' SIGNATURE ON THIS, NOW - HE'LL LOSE MILLIONS!!

BIG JULIUS CANNOT BE DISTOIBED!! - HE IS NOW INVOLVED WIT' A MATTER WHICH MEANS MORE TO HIM THAN POWER, WEALTH, OR EVEN DOLLS!!

IN THE BOMBPROOF STUDY -

URPSIES PRESENTS MILTON, THE MASKED MARTIAN

THE ANNOUNCER SPEAKS - "THE FROG-MAN, FROM SATURN, AND THE MOOSE-MAN FROM THE MOON, ARE PLOTTING TO MASSACRE THE SIMPLE PRUNE-PEOPLE, FROM PLUTO!!"

DEM CREEPS!! - DEY WON'T SUCCEED!! - I GOT FAIT' IN MILTON!!

WE'LL STEW THOSE PRUNE-PEOPLE WITH THIS SPACE-GUN!!

- AND THEN WE'LL TAKE OVER THE PRUNE'S PLANET!! THAT'LL BE A PLUM.!!

STOP!! - YOU UNEARTHLY MONSTERS!!

IT'S MILTON, THE MASKED MARTIAN!!

HE'S SUPERIOR TO US INCREDIBLE CREATURES FROM STRANGE PLANETS!! HE DOESN'T NEED SPACE-SHIPS TO FLY WITH!!

HE CAN FLY, BY WILL POWER, ALONE.!! -

WELL, THAT'S THE LATEST WRINKLE WITH THE PRUNE-PEOPLE!! - AND, IF YOU, MY LITTLE PALS, WANT TO BE AS POWERFUL AS I AM - EAT URPSIES!! -

I'M EATIN' 'EM, MILTON - SEE?

- AND, AS MILTON ZOOMS OFF, LET'S ONCE AGAIN RE-AFFIRM OUR FAITH IN THE MASKED MARTIAN. LITTLE PALS!! - DO YOU BELIEVE IN MILTON, OR DON'T YOU?

I BELIEVE!! I GOT FAIT'!!

AT THAT MOMENT - IN DOGPATCH -

AH DIDN'T WIN NO PRIZE AT TH' FOURTH GRADE HISTORICAL CHARACTER PARTY!!

THET IGGORANT TEACHER CLAIMS THAR'S NO SECH HISTORICAL CHARACTER AS MILTON, THE MASKED MARTIAN!!

OH, NO? - WAIT, AND SEE!!

Al Capp

Tm. Reg. U. S. Pat. Off. — All rights reserved Cop. 1955 by United Feature Syndicate, Inc.   11-27

LI'L ABNER by Al Capp

AH DIDN'T **WIN** NO PRIZE IN TH' FOURTH GRADE "HISTORICAL CHARACTER" CONTEST—

—ON ACCOUNT THET IGGORANT TEACHER CLAIMED THAR **WARN'T** NO SECH HISTORICAL CHARACTER AS **MILTON TH' MASKED MARTIAN!!**

SHECKS!!—EV'RY CHILE WHUT LOOKS AT TV **KNOWS** THAR'S A MILTON— AN' **HE KIN FLY!!**—

AT THE CARNIVAL, NEARBY—

GET HER DOWN!!!

F-FORGIVE ME, O COLD-EYED ONE!! I AM NEW AT THIS LEVITATION RACKET!!—GETTING THEM **UP**—AH, 'TIS CHILD'S PLAY!!—

SWAMI RIVA AND ASSISTANT **OLMAN RIVA** HINDU MAGIC

BUT—**GULP!**—GETTING THEM **DOWN**—ALAS!!—I FEAR I HAVE NOT MASTERED THAT!!—

LET'S **TAR AN' FEATHER HIM!!**

GREETINGS, MY BRILLIANT YOUNG APPRENTICE!!—AND HOW WENT YOUR FIRST DAY, TAKING MY PLACE AT THE CARNIVAL?

LO!!—IT WENT **ILL**, OLD MASTER!!

I GOT ONE **UP**, ALL RIGHT, BUT WHEN IT CAME TO GETTING HER **DOWN**—ALAS!! I HAD **FORGOTTEN** THE PROPER PROCEDURE!!

SHE **STILL** IS UP THERE, AND I BARELY ESCAPED WITH MY WRETCHED LIFE!!—

OX!!—COCKROACH! WATCH CLOSELY!! YOU GET THEM UP— **THIS** WAY!!

YES, YES!! THAT I HAVE MASTERED, MASTER···

—AND YOU GET THEM DOWN, SIMPLY BY—?.?.

THERE THEY ARE!!

HEY!!—DON'T LEAVE ME UP HERE!!

Sunday Mirror

19 COMICS

15¢

NEW YORK, N. Y. SUNDAY, DECEMBER 11, 1955

LI'L ABNER by Al Capp

Sunday Mirror

19 COMICS 15¢

NEW YORK, N.Y. SUNDAY, DECEMBER 18, 1955

LI'L ABNER by Al Capp

A CHRISTMAS MESSAGE FROM A TIMELESS PAINTING

Magazine Section

Sunday Mirror
NEW YORK, N. Y. SUNDAY, DECEMBER 25, 1955

19 COMICS   15¢

LI'L ABNER by Al Capp

9

LI'L ABNER *School daze!!~* BY AL CAPP

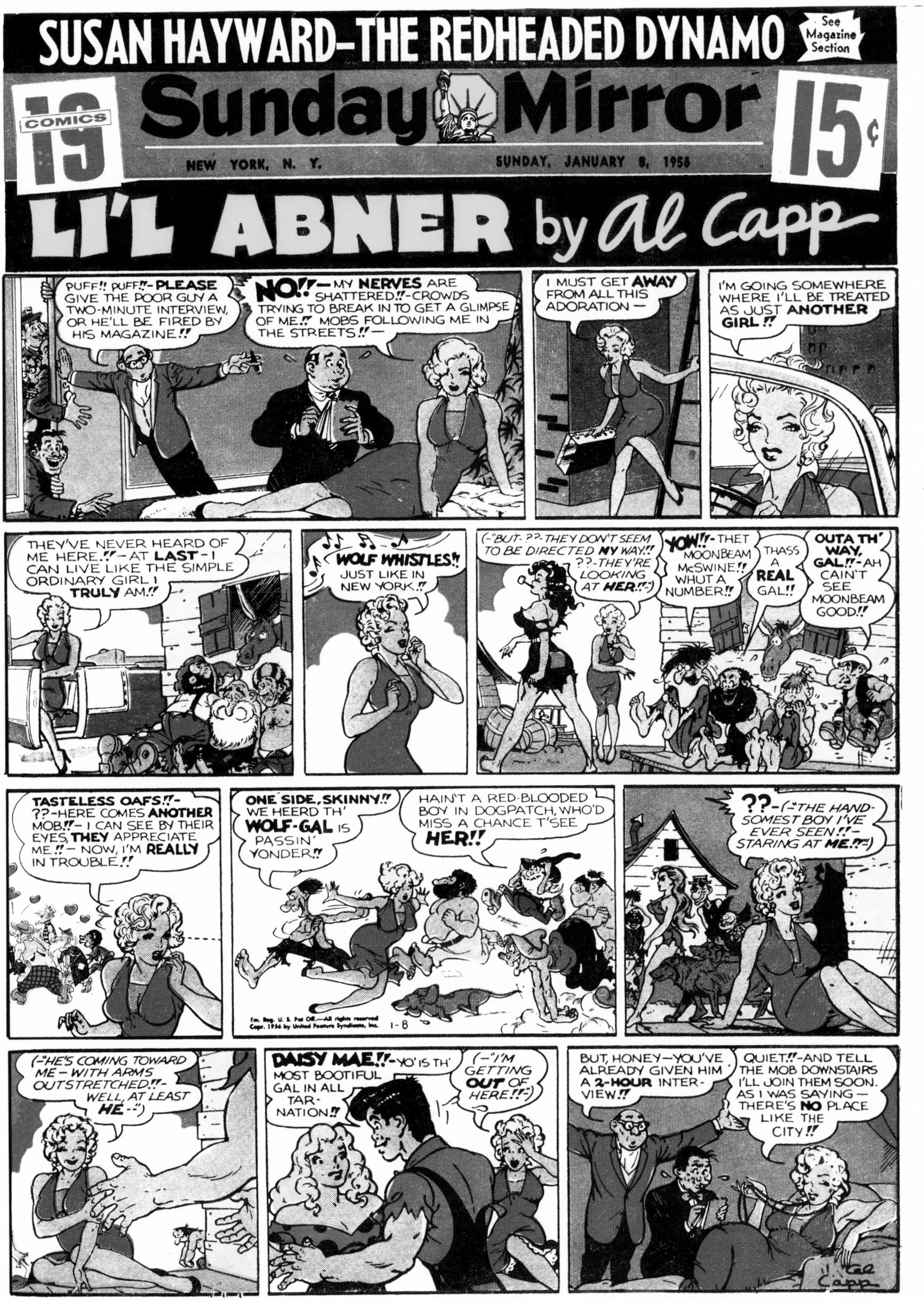
SUSAN HAYWARD–THE REDHEADED DYNAMO
See Magazine Section
19 COMICS
Sunday Mirror
15¢
NEW YORK, N. Y.
SUNDAY, JANUARY 8, 1956
LI'L ABNER by Al Capp
PUFF!! PUFF!!–PLEASE GIVE THE POOR GUY A TWO-MINUTE INTERVIEW, OR HE'LL BE FIRED BY HIS MAGAZINE!!
NO!!–MY NERVES ARE SHATTERED!!–CROWDS TRYING TO BREAK IN TO GET A GLIMPSE OF ME!! MOBS FOLLOWING ME IN THE STREETS!!–
I MUST GET AWAY FROM ALL THIS ADORATION–
I'M GOING SOMEWHERE WHERE I'LL BE TREATED AS JUST ANOTHER GIRL!!
THEY'VE NEVER HEARD OF ME HERE!!–AT LAST–I CAN LIVE LIKE THE SIMPLE ORDINARY GIRL I TRULY AM!!
WOLF WHISTLES!! JUST LIKE IN NEW YORK!!
(–"BUT–??–THEY DON'T SEEM TO BE DIRECTED MY WAY!! ??–THEY'RE LOOKING AT HER!!"–)
YOW!!–THET MOONBEAM McSWINE!! WHUT A NUMBER!!
THASS A REAL GAL!!
OUTA TH' WAY, GAL!!–AH CAIN'T SEE MOONBEAM GOOD!!
TASTELESS OAFS!!–??–HERE COMES ANOTHER MOB!!–I CAN SEE BY THEIR EYES, THEY APPRECIATE ME!!–NOW, I'M REALLY IN TROUBLE!!
ONE SIDE, SKINNY!! WE HEERD TH' WOLF-GAL IS PASSIN' YONDER!!
HAIN'T A RED-BLOODED BOY IN DOGPATCH, WHO'D MISS A CHANCE T'SEE HER!!
Tm. Reg. U. S. Pat Off.—All rights reserved
Copr. 1956 by United Feature Syndicate, Inc.
1-8
??–(–"THE HANDSOMEST BOY I'VE EVER SEEN!!–STARING AT ME!!"–)
(–"HE'S COMING TOWARD ME–WITH ARMS OUTSTRETCHED!!–WELL, AT LEAST HE–")
DAISY MAE!!–YO' IS TH' MOST BOOTIFUL GAL IN ALL TAR-NATION!!
(–"I'M GETTING OUT OF HERE!!"–)
BUT, HONEY–YOU'VE ALREADY GIVEN HIM A 2-HOUR INTER-VIEW!!
QUIET!!–AND TELL THE MOB DOWNSTAIRS I'LL JOIN THEM SOON. AS I WAS SAYING–THERE'S NO PLACE LIKE THE CITY!!
Al Capp

GIRLS! HERE'S FASTEST WAY TO GET MARRIED
See Magazine Section
 COMICS 19
Sunday Mirror 15¢
NEW YORK, N. Y. SUNDAY, JANUARY 15, 1956

LI'L ABNER by Al Capp

19 COMICS

Sunday Mirror

15¢

NEW YORK, N. Y.   SUNDAY, JANUARY 22, 1956

LI'L ABNER by Al Capp

Sunday Mirror

18 COMICS

15¢

NEW YORK, N. Y.

SUNDAY, JANUARY 29, 1956

LI'L ABNER by Al Capp

14

LI'L ABNER by Al Capp

Ye World's Rarest Recipes—no. 89
Ye Fabled Ecstasy Sauce!!——
Boil ye one Hammus Alabammus (if thou art fortunate enough to possess one) for hours and hours and hours—until ye succulent beastie simmereth down to one Delicious Drop——
Lo!!—Tis Ecstasy Sauce!!—

—IF I CAN GET SALOMEY FOR CRAWLEY VAN GROPE—

HE CAN MAKE HER INTO ECSTASY SAUCE—

GET INTO THE GOURMET'S CLUB—

—AND MARRY ME!!

IF I CAN KEEP SALOMEY FROM CRAWLEY—

HE CAN'T MAKE ECSTASY SAUCE—

HE WON'T GET INTO THE GOURMET'S CLUB—

—AND HE'LL BE SO HUMILIATED—

HE'LL MARRY ME!!

IS EVERYBODY IN TH' CITY DRESSIN' THET WAY, NOW?—AH-GULP!!—HAIN'T BIN TO TH' CITY IN SECH A LONG TIME, MAMMY—

SHOOSH!!—

I DASHED OUT OF THE CLUB, AS SOON AS I THOUGHT OF IT!!—I'M TIRED OF TANGOING WITH TIGERS.

I'VE GOT A GREAT IDEA FOR A NEW ACT!!—A JIG WITH A PIG!!

HMM—

THINK OF IT!!—FAME, FORTUNE, APPLAUSE, PUBLICITY!! EVERYTHING A PIG WANTS!!—AND, OH!!—THE PEOPLE SHE'LL MEET!!—JOSE FERRER, TYRONE POWER, JACKIE GLEASON, HENNY YOUNGMAN——

HENNY YOUNGMAN? THET SETTLES IT!!—SHE KIN GO!!—

(—ONCE ON THE PLANE AND OVER THE MOUNTAINS, I'LL DROP HER!!—)

STOP!!—

IT'S BESSIE!!

WHUT BRINGS YO' A-SHAMBLIN' HOME ON YORE CREAKY OLE LAIGS, ELDER SISTER?

GIVE ME THAT PIG, YOU MURDERESS!!

SHE MEANT TO KILL SALOMEY!!—I'LL TAKE HER BACK TO NEW YORK, AND KEEP HER OUT OF HOT WATER!!—

YOU MEAN TOSS HER INTO HOT WATER!!—AND BOIL HER, AND BOIL HER, UNTIL ALL THAT'S LEFT IS ONE DELICIOUS DROP!!

MAH SISTER WOULDN'T DO NOTHIN' LIKE THET!! GO BACK AN' TANGO WIF YORE TIGER—AFORE YO' TANGOS WIF ME!!

2-5

19 COMICS — **Sunday Mirror** — **15¢**

NEW YORK, N. Y. — SUNDAY, FEBRUARY 12, 1956

LI'L ABNER by Al Capp

Sunday Mirror

COMICS 19

15¢

NEW YORK, N. Y.   SUNDAY, FEBRUARY 19, 1956

LI'L ABNER by Al Capp

WITHOUT **YOU** TO MAKE ECSTASY SAUCE OF, CRAWLEY WILL BE TOSSED OUT OF THE GOURMET'S CLUB — AND INTO MY ARMS!!

AT THE GOURMET'S CLUB — THE GREAT MOMENT ARRIVES!! —

GENTLEMEN!! — ROAST RUMP OF WARBLING RHINOCEROS, WITH ECSTASY SAUCE!! —

MAGNIFICENT!! SUBLIME!! BRAVO!!

I CONGRATULATE YOU — MEMBER VAN GROPE!!

AND NOW — A **STANDING OVATION**, FOR ARMAND, THE CHEF!!

ARMAND!! ARMAND!! COME **IN**, YOU FAT, JUICY, LITTLE GENIUS!!

GENTLEMEN!! — I AM PIERRE, ZE ASSISTANT TO ARMAND. I 'AVE FOR YOU, ZE NEWS **SAD**!!

ZE LAST LIVING HAMMUS ALABAMMUS WAS ZE **PRICE** ARMAND WAS ASKED TO PAY FOR A KISS FROM A CERTAIN LADY'S WINE-RED LIPS!!

BEING A TRUE FRENCHMAN, 'E **PAID**!! —

BUT — ??. **WHAT** DID HE MAKE THIS — YUM!! ECSTASY SAUCE OF ?

PLEASE, GENTLEMEN!! — I CANNOT GO ON !! — PAUVRE JUICY LEETLE ARMAND!! — 'E DEED NOT LET YOU DOWN !!

Society News

IT'S A BIG DAY FOR CRAWLEY VAN GROPE !!

Admitted to exclusive Gourmet's Club, and weds winsome widow on same day !! —

2-19

MANY HAPPY RETURNS!!

WELCOME BACK TO YORE MAMMY'S ARMS, SALOMEY, DEAR!!

19 COMICS   Sunday Mirror   15¢
NEW YORK, N. Y.   SUNDAY, FEBRUARY 26, 1956

LI'L ABNER by Al Capp

Sunday Mirror

19 COMICS   15¢

NEW YORK, N. Y.   SUNDAY, MARCH 4, 1956

LI'L ABNER by Al Capp

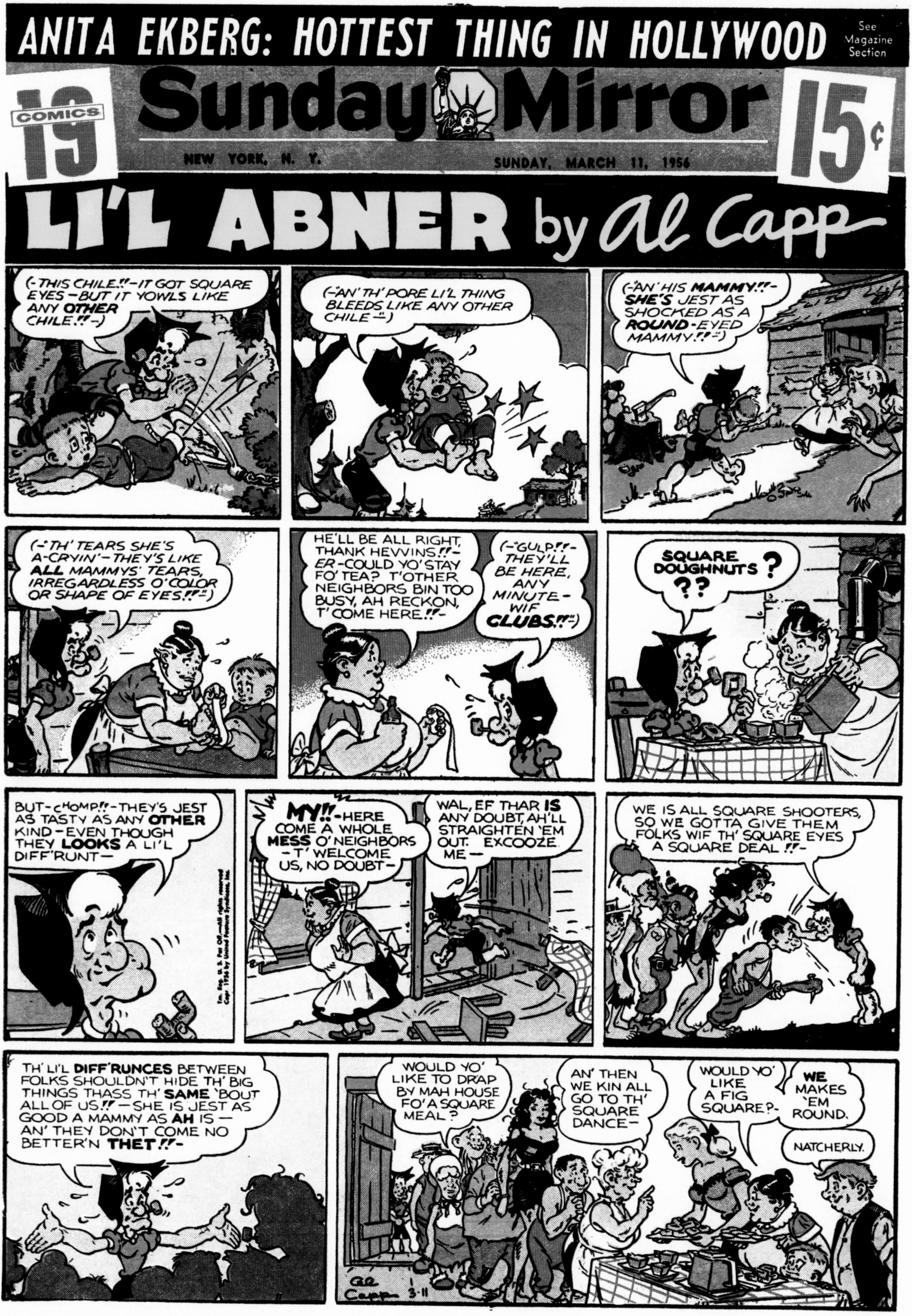
ANITA EKBERG: HOTTEST THING IN HOLLYWOOD
See Magazine Section
Sunday Mirror
COMICS 19
15¢
NEW YORK, N. Y.
SUNDAY, MARCH 11, 1956
LI'L ABNER by Al Capp
(-THIS CHILE!!-IT GOT SQUARE EYES-BUT IT YOWLS LIKE ANY OTHER CHILE!!-)
(-AN' TH' PORE LI'L THING BLEEDS LIKE ANY OTHER CHILE-)
(-AN' HIS MAMMY!!-SHE'S JEST AS SHOCKED AS A ROUND-EYED MAMMY!!-)
(-TH' TEARS SHE'S A-CRYIN'-THEY'S LIKE ALL MAMMYS' TEARS, IRREGARDLESS O'COLOR OR SHAPE OF EYES!!-)
HE'LL BE ALL RIGHT, THANK HEVVINS!!-ER-COULD YO' STAY FO' TEA? T'OTHER NEIGHBORS BIN TOO BUSY, AH RECKON, T' COME HERE!!-
(-GULP!!-THEY'LL BE HERE, ANY MINUTE-WIF CLUBS!!-)
SQUARE DOUGHNUTS ???
BUT-CHOMP!!-THEY'S JEST AS TASTY AS ANY OTHER KIND-EVEN THOUGH THEY LOOKS A LI'L DIFF'RUNT-
MY!!-HERE COME A WHOLE MESS O' NEIGHBORS-T' WELCOME US, NO DOUBT-
WAL, EF THAR IS ANY DOUBT, AH'LL STRAIGHTEN 'EM OUT. EXCOOZE ME-
WE IS ALL SQUARE SHOOTERS, SO WE GOTTA GIVE THEM FOLKS WIF TH' SQUARE EYES A SQUARE DEAL!!-
TH' LI'L DIFF'RUNCES BETWEEN FOLKS SHOULDN'T HIDE TH' BIG THINGS THASS TH' SAME 'BOUT ALL OF US!!-SHE IS JEST AS GOOD A MAMMY AS AH IS-AN' THEY DON'T COME NO BETTER'N THET!!-
WOULD YO' LIKE TO DRAP BY MAH HOUSE FO' A SQUARE MEAL?
AN' THEN WE KIN ALL GO TO TH' SQUARE DANCE-
WOULD YO' LIKE A FIG SQUARE?-
WE MAKES 'EM ROUND.
NATCHERLY.
Al Capp 3-11

Sunday Mirror

19 COMICS

15¢

NEW YORK, N. Y.   SUNDAY, MARCH 18, 1956

LI'L ABNER *by Al Capp*

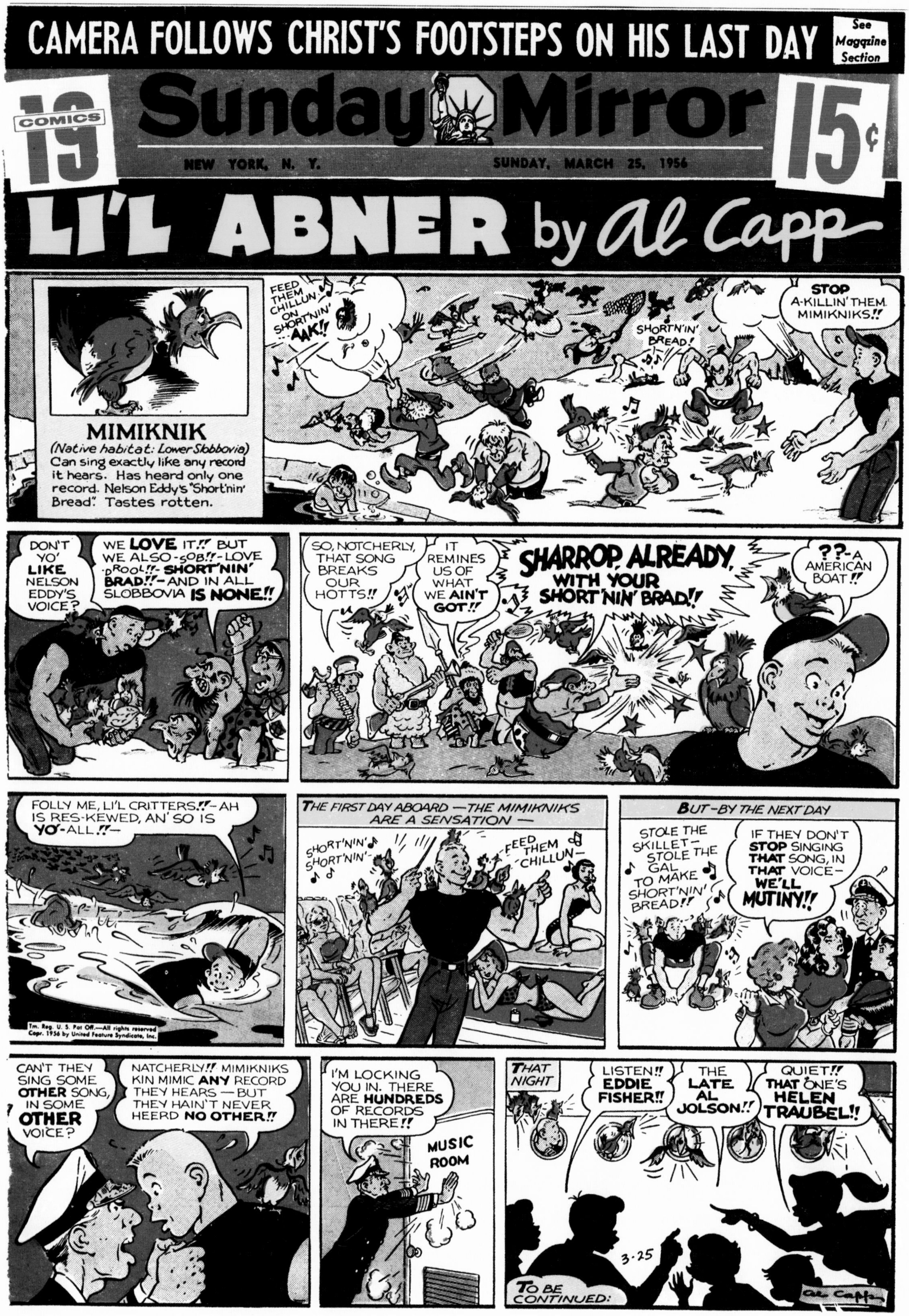

CAMERA FOLLOWS CHRIST'S FOOTSTEPS ON HIS LAST DAY
See Magazine Section
19 COMICS
Sunday Mirror
15¢
NEW YORK, N. Y.
SUNDAY, MARCH 25, 1956
LI'L ABNER by Al Capp
MIMIKNIK
(Native habitat: Lower Slobbovia) Can sing exactly like any record it hears. Has heard only one record. Nelson Eddy's "Short'nin' Bread". Tastes rotten.
FEED THEM CHILLUN ON SHORT'NIN'-AAK!!
SHORT'NIN' BREAD!
STOP A-KILLIN' THEM MIMIKNIKS!!
DON'T YO' LIKE NELSON EDDY'S VOICE?
WE LOVE IT!! BUT WE ALSO-SOB!!-LOVE -DROOL!!- SHORT'NIN' BRAD!!-AND IN ALL SLOBBOVIA IS NONE!!
SO, NOTCHERLY, THAT SONG BREAKS OUR HOTTS!!
IT REMINES US OF WHAT WE AIN'T GOT!!
SHARROP, ALREADY, WITH YOUR SHORT'NIN' BRAD!!
??-A AMERICAN BOAT!!
FOLLY ME, LI'L CRITTERS!!-AH IS RES-KEWED, AN' SO IS YO'-ALL!!-
Tm. Reg. U. S. Pat Off.—All rights reserved Copr. 1956 by United Feature Syndicate, Inc.
THE FIRST DAY ABOARD —THE MIMIKNIKS ARE A SENSATION—
SHORT'NIN' SHORT'NIN'-
FEED THEM CHILLUN-
BUT-BY THE NEXT DAY
STOLE THE SKILLET-STOLE THE GAL TO MAKE SHORT'NIN' BREAD!!
IF THEY DON'T STOP SINGING THAT SONG, IN THAT VOICE- WE'LL MUTINY!!
CAN'T THEY SING SOME OTHER SONG, IN SOME OTHER VOICE?
NATCHERLY!! MIMIKNIKS KIN MIMIC ANY RECORD THEY HEARS — BUT THEY HAIN'T NEVER HEERD NO OTHER!!
I'M LOCKING YOU IN. THERE ARE HUNDREDS OF RECORDS IN THERE!!
MUSIC ROOM
THAT NIGHT
LISTEN!! EDDIE FISHER!!
THE LATE AL JOLSON!!
QUIET!! THAT ONE'S HELEN TRAUBEL!!
3-25
TO BE CONTINUED:

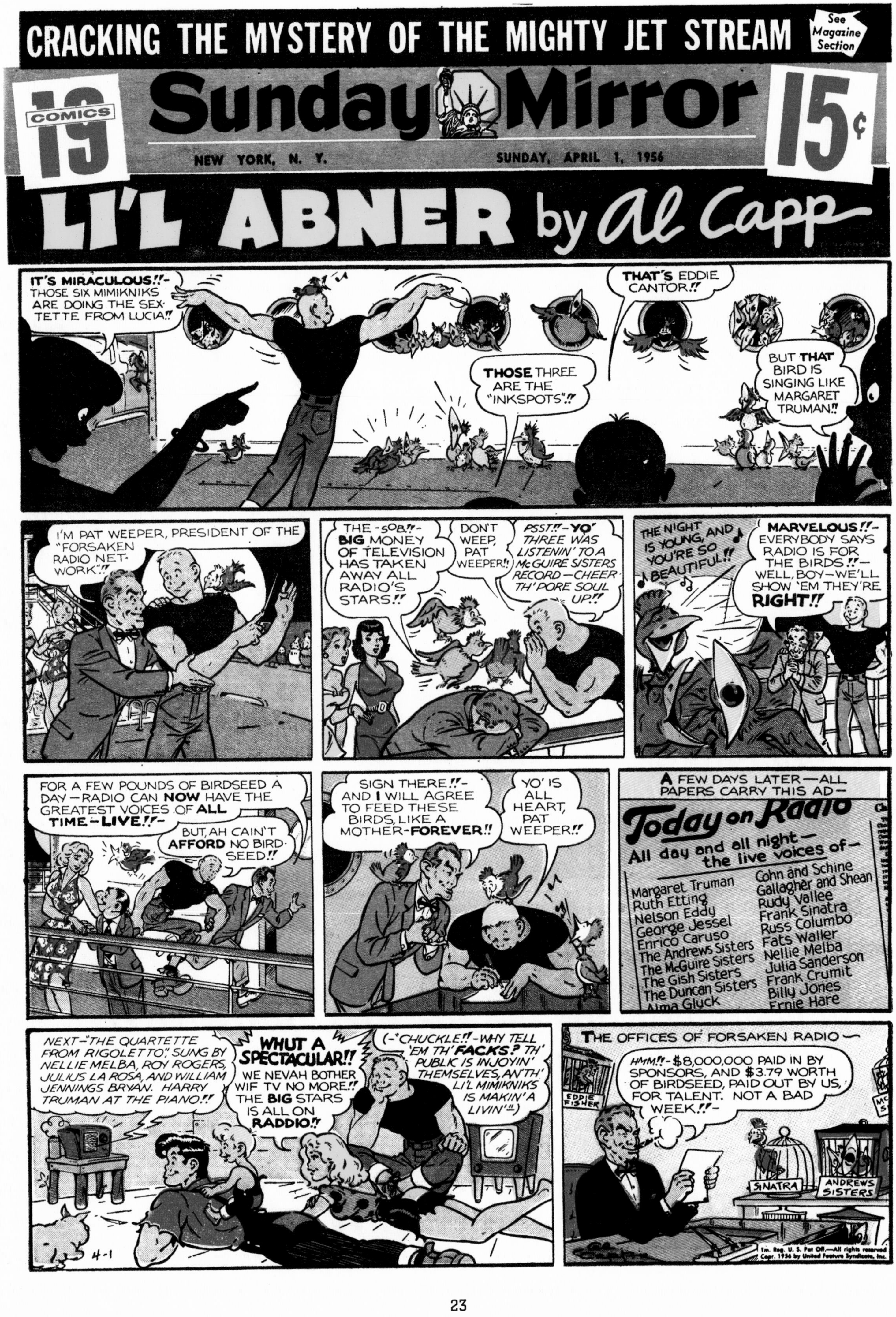

CRACKING THE MYSTERY OF THE MIGHTY JET STREAM
See Magazine Section
19 COMICS
Sunday Mirror
15¢
NEW YORK, N. Y.
SUNDAY, APRIL 1, 1956
LI'L ABNER by Al Capp
IT'S MIRACULOUS!!- THOSE SIX MIMIKNIKS ARE DOING THE SEXTETTE FROM LUCIA!!
THAT'S EDDIE CANTOR!!
THOSE THREE ARE THE "INKSPOTS"!!
BUT THAT BIRD IS SINGING LIKE MARGARET TRUMAN!!
I'M PAT WEEPER, PRESIDENT OF THE "FORSAKEN RADIO NETWORK"!!
THE -SOB!!- BIG MONEY OF TELEVISION HAS TAKEN AWAY ALL RADIO'S STARS!!
DON'T WEEP, PAT WEEPER!!
PSST!!-YO' THREE WAS LISTENIN' TO A McGUIRE SISTERS RECORD-CHEER TH'PORE SOUL UP!!
THE NIGHT IS YOUNG, AND YOU'RE SO BEAUTIFUL!!
MARVELOUS!!- EVERYBODY SAYS RADIO IS FOR THE BIRDS!!- WELL, BOY-WE'LL SHOW 'EM THEY'RE RIGHT!!
FOR A FEW POUNDS OF BIRDSEED A DAY-RADIO CAN NOW HAVE THE GREATEST VOICES OF ALL TIME-LIVE!!-
BUT, AH CAIN'T AFFORD NO BIRD-SEED!!
SIGN THERE!!- AND I WILL AGREE TO FEED THESE BIRDS, LIKE A MOTHER-FOREVER!!
YO'IS ALL HEART, PAT WEEPER!!
A FEW DAYS LATER-ALL PAPERS CARRY THIS AD-
Today on Radio
All day and all night- the live voices of-
Margaret Truman
Ruth Etting
Nelson Eddy
George Jessel
Enrico Caruso
The Andrews Sisters
The McGuire Sisters
The Gish Sisters
The Duncan Sisters
Alma Gluck
Cohn and Schine
Gallagher and Shean
Rudy Vallee
Frank Sinatra
Russ Columbo
Fats Waller
Nellie Melba
Julia Sanderson
Frank Crumit
Billy Jones
Ernie Hare
NEXT-"THE QUARTETTE FROM RIGOLETTO," SUNG BY NELLIE MELBA, ROY ROGERS, JULIUS LA ROSA, AND WILLIAM JENNINGS BRYAN. HARRY TRUMAN AT THE PIANO!!
WHUT A SPECTACULAR!! WE NEVAH BOTHER WIF TV NO MORE!! THE BIG STARS IS ALL ON RADDIO!!
(-'CHUCKLE!!-WHY TELL 'EM TH' FACKS? TH' PUBLIC IS INJOYIN' THEMSELVES, AN'TH' LI'L MIMIKNIKS IS MAKIN' A LIVIN'!!-)
4-1
THE OFFICES OF FORSAKEN RADIO-
EDDIE FISHER
HMM!!-$8,000,000 PAID IN BY SPONSORS, AND $3.79 WORTH OF BIRDSEED, PAID OUT BY US, FOR TALENT. NOT A BAD WEEK!!-
SINATRA
ANDREWS SISTERS
Tm. Reg. U. S. Pat. Off.—All rights reserved
Copr. 1956 by United Feature Syndicate, Inc.

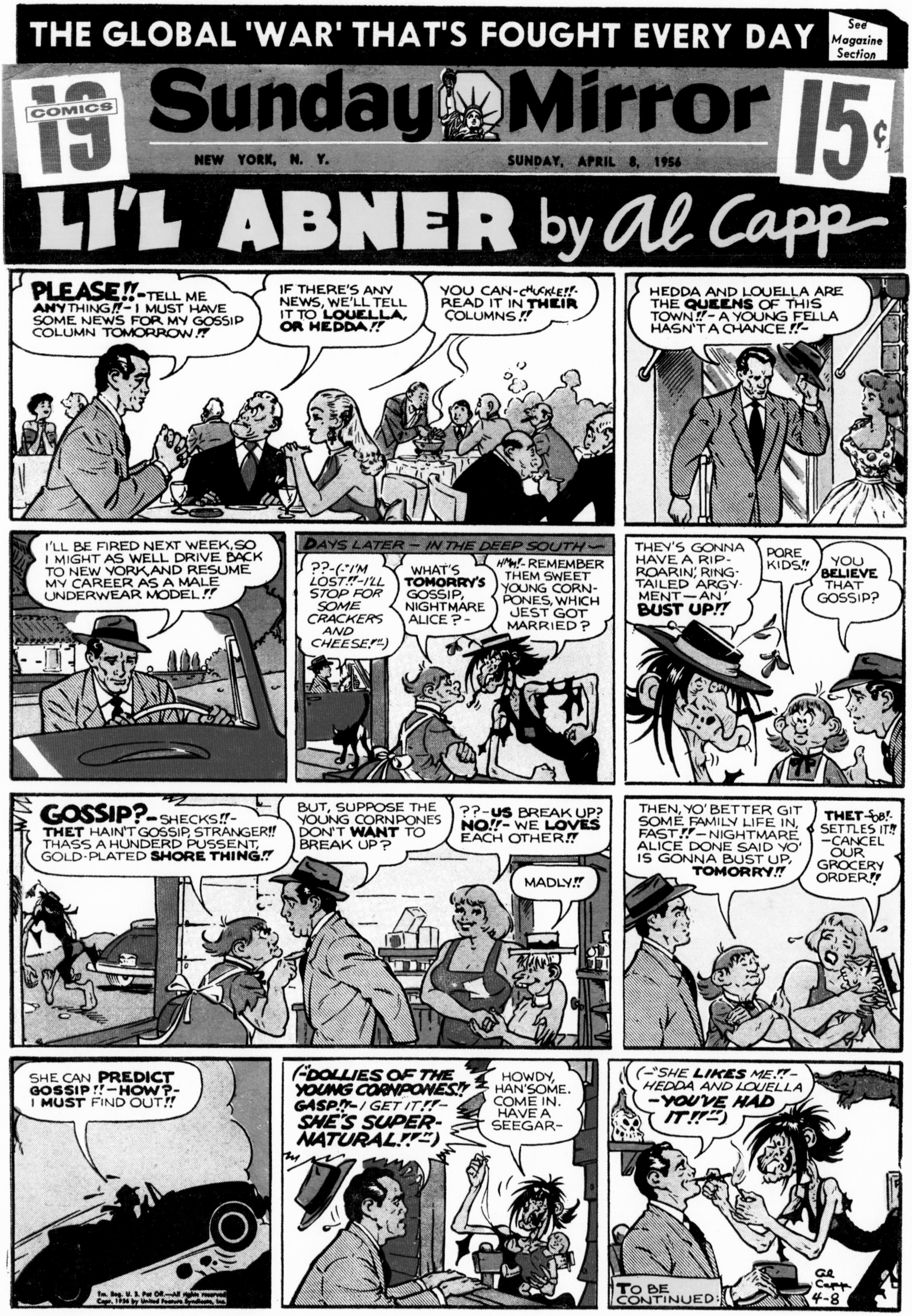
THE GLOBAL 'WAR' THAT'S FOUGHT EVERY DAY
See Magazine Section
19 COMICS
Sunday Mirror
15¢
NEW YORK, N. Y.
SUNDAY, APRIL 8, 1956
LI'L ABNER by Al Capp
PLEASE!!-TELL ME ANYTHING!!-I MUST HAVE SOME NEWS FOR MY GOSSIP COLUMN TOMORROW!!
IF THERE'S ANY NEWS, WE'LL TELL IT TO LOUELLA, OR HEDDA!!
YOU CAN-CHUCKLE!!-READ IT IN THEIR COLUMNS!!
HEDDA AND LOUELLA ARE THE QUEENS OF THIS TOWN!!-A YOUNG FELLA HASN'T A CHANCE!!-
I'LL BE FIRED NEXT WEEK, SO I MIGHT AS WELL DRIVE BACK TO NEW YORK, AND RESUME MY CAREER AS A MALE UNDERWEAR MODEL!!
DAYS LATER — IN THE DEEP SOUTH —
??-("I'M LOST!!-I'LL STOP FOR SOME CRACKERS AND CHEESE!"-)
WHAT'S TOMORRY'S GOSSIP, NIGHTMARE ALICE?-
HMM!-REMEMBER THEM SWEET YOUNG CORNPONES, WHICH JEST GOT MARRIED?
THEY'S GONNA HAVE A RIP-ROARIN', RING-TAILED ARGY-MENT—AN' BUST UP!!
PORE KIDS!!
YOU BELIEVE THAT GOSSIP?
GOSSIP?-SHECKS!!-THET HAIN'T GOSSIP, STRANGER!! THASS A HUNDERD PUSSENT, GOLD-PLATED SHORE THING!!
BUT, SUPPOSE THE YOUNG CORNPONES DON'T WANT TO BREAK UP?
??-US BREAK UP? NO!!-WE LOVES EACH OTHER!!
MADLY!!
THEN, YO' BETTER GIT SOME FAMILY LIFE IN, FAST!!-NIGHTMARE ALICE DONE SAID YO' IS GONNA BUST UP, TOMORRY!!
THET-SOB!-SETTLES IT!!-CANCEL OUR GROCERY ORDER!!
SHE CAN PREDICT GOSSIP!!-HOW?-I MUST FIND OUT!!
(-"DOLLIES OF THE YOUNG CORNPONES!!" GASP!!-I GET IT!!-SHE'S SUPER-NATURAL!!"-)
HOWDY, HAN'SOME. COME IN. HAVE A SEEGAR-
(-"SHE LIKES ME!!-HEDDA AND LOUELLA -YOU'VE HAD IT!!"-)
TO BE CONTINUED:
Al Capp 4-8

LI'L ABNER
by
AL CAPP ®

(-!! THIS CREEPY OLD CRONE CAN **MAKE** THINGS HAPPEN TO PEOPLE.!!- WITH **HER** AS MY ASSISTANT---)

(-"I'D BE THE **GREATEST** HOLLYWOOD COLUMNIST!! IF **I** PREDICTED PINKY LEE WOULD KNOCK OUT ROCKY MARCIANO, AT CIRO'S---)

(-"SHE COULD **MAKE** IT HAPPEN.!!-I'D HAVE THE EXCLUSIVE.!!-) THAT'S A FINE CIGAR, DEAR.!!

ALLUS SMOKES 'EM MAH-SELF!!

ODD AROMA!! WHAT ARE THEY MADE OF?

EF AH TOLE YO', YO'D DROP DAID.!!

AX NO QUESTIONS. JEST INJOY IT, LIKE **AH** IS INJOYIN' HAVIN' A HAN'SOME YOUNG FELLA, LIKE **YO**,' CALLIN' ON ME.

IT GITS MIGHTY LONE-SOME HERE–ALTHOUGH MAH BATS AN' LIZARDS **IS** CHEERFUL COMP'NY. AH GOT EV'RYTHING AH WANTS, 'CEPT-GULP!!- **ONE** THING !!

MONEY?

NO-**LOVE**!!-AH KIN CONJURE UP **EVERY-THING ELSE**.!!- BUT, AH IS A GAL-WIF A HEART CHOCKFULL O' GIRLISH DREAMS, AN' YEARNIN'S!!

THEN, THE PLACE FOR YOU, MY DEAR –IS **HOLLYWOOD**!!

IT'S CHOCKFULL OF THE HANDSOMEST MEN IN THE WORLD!! CARY GRANT, ROCK HUDSON, RORY CALHOUN, G. DAVID SCHINE–

G. DAVID SCHINE?

YOU'RE A SWEET KID. I'LL GIVE YOU A BREAK.!!

YOU CAN COME TO HOLLYWOOD, AS MY ASSISTANT. ALL YOU HAVE TO DO, IS…

4-15

–MAKE ALL MY COLUMN PREDICTIONS COME TRUE !!-

IS **THET** ALL? **LE'S GO**.!!

TO BE CONTINUED:

25

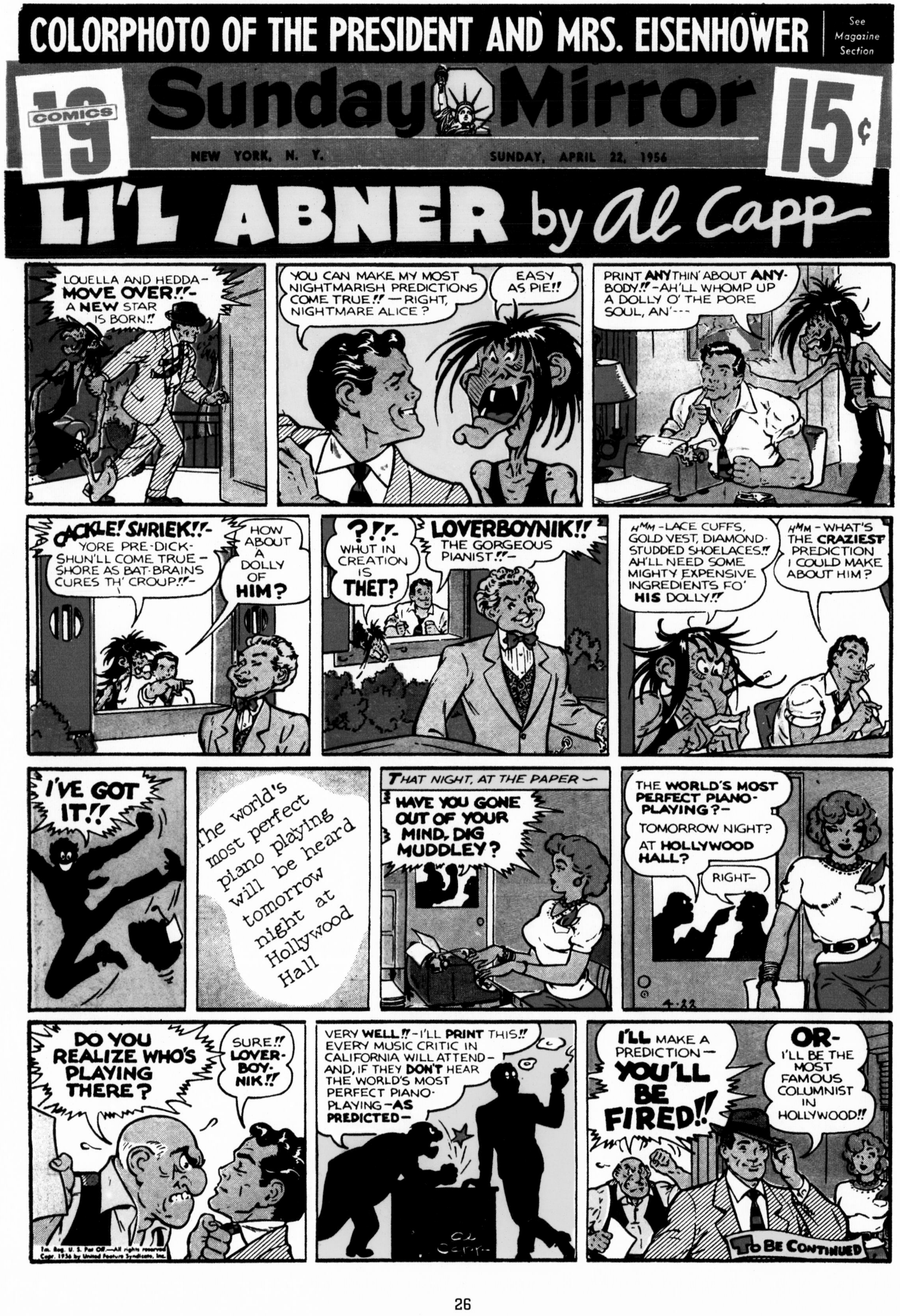
COLORPHOTO OF THE PRESIDENT AND MRS. EISENHOWER
See Magazine Section
19 COMICS
Sunday Mirror
15¢
NEW YORK, N. Y.
SUNDAY, APRIL 22, 1956
LI'L ABNER by Al Capp
LOUELLA AND HEDDA- MOVE OVER!!- A NEW STAR IS BORN!!
YOU CAN MAKE MY MOST NIGHTMARISH PREDICTIONS COME TRUE!! —RIGHT, NIGHTMARE ALICE?
EASY AS PIE!!
PRINT ANYTHIN' ABOUT ANYBODY!!-AH'LL WHOMP UP A DOLLY O' THE PORE SOUL, AN'---
CACKLE! SHRIEK!!- YORE PRE-DICK-SHUN'LL COME TRUE- SHORE AS BAT-BRAINS CURES TH' CROUP!!-
HOW ABOUT A DOLLY OF HIM?
?!!- WHUT IN CREATION IS THET?
LOVERBOYNIK!! THE GORGEOUS PIANIST!!-
HMM-LACE CUFFS, GOLD VEST, DIAMOND-STUDDED SHOELACES!! AH'LL NEED SOME MIGHTY EXPENSIVE INGREDIENTS FO' HIS DOLLY!!
HMM-WHAT'S THE CRAZIEST PREDICTION I COULD MAKE ABOUT HIM?
I'VE GOT IT!!
The world's most perfect piano playing will be heard tomorrow night at Hollywood Hall
THAT NIGHT, AT THE PAPER—
HAVE YOU GONE OUT OF YOUR MIND, DIG MUDDLEY?
THE WORLD'S MOST PERFECT PIANO-PLAYING?-
TOMORROW NIGHT?
AT HOLLYWOOD HALL?
RIGHT-
4-22
DO YOU REALIZE WHO'S PLAYING THERE?
SURE!! LOVER-BOY-NIK!!
VERY WELL!!-I'LL PRINT THIS!! EVERY MUSIC CRITIC IN CALIFORNIA WILL ATTEND- AND, IF THEY DON'T HEAR THE WORLD'S MOST PERFECT PIANO-PLAYING-AS PREDICTED-
I'LL MAKE A PREDICTION- YOU'LL BE FIRED!!
OR- I'LL BE THE MOST FAMOUS COLUMNIST IN HOLLYWOOD!!
Tm. Reg. U. S. Pat. Off.—All rights reserved Copr. 1956 by United Feature Syndicate, Inc.
Al Capp
TO BE CONTINUED

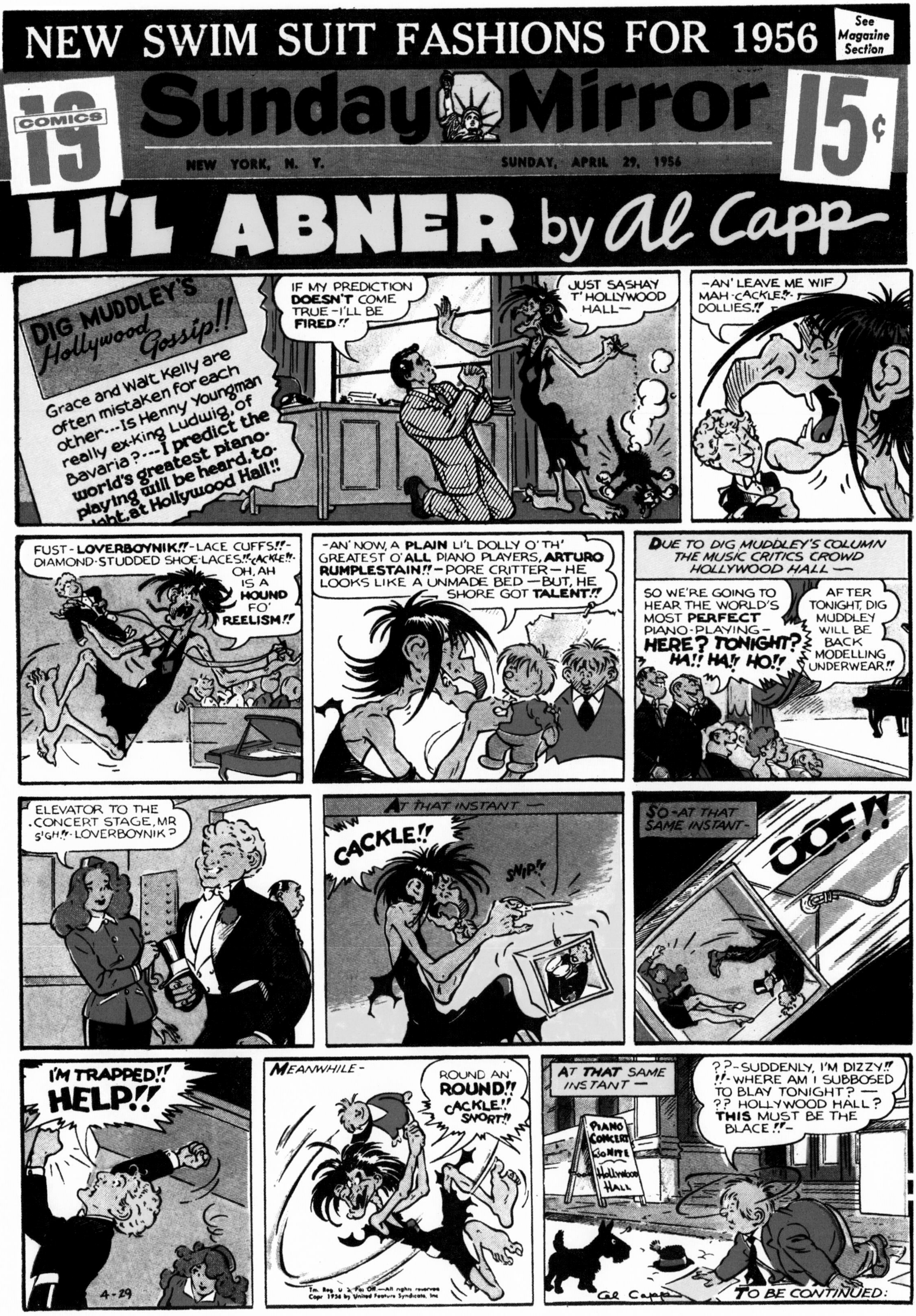

NEW SWIM SUIT FASHIONS FOR 1956
See Magazine Section
19 COMICS
Sunday Mirror
15¢
NEW YORK, N. Y.
SUNDAY, APRIL 29, 1956
LI'L ABNER by Al Capp
DIG MUDDLEY'S Hollywood Gossip!!
Grace and Walt Kelly are often mistaken for each other---Is Henny Youngman really ex-King Ludwig, of Bavaria?---I predict the world's greatest piano-playing will be heard, to-
ight, at Hollywood Hall!!
IF MY PREDICTION DOESN'T COME TRUE - I'LL BE FIRED!!
JUST SASHAY T' HOLLYWOOD HALL—
-AN' LEAVE ME WIF MAH-CACKLE!!- DOLLIES!!
FUST-LOVERBOYNIK!!-LACE CUFFS!!- DIAMOND-STUDDED SHOE-LACES!!-CACKLE!!- OH, AH IS A HOUND FO' REELISM!!
-AN' NOW, A PLAIN LI'L DOLLY O' TH' GREATEST O' ALL PIANO PLAYERS, ARTURO RUMPLESTAIN!!-PORE CRITTER-HE LOOKS LIKE A UNMADE BED-BUT, HE SHORE GOT TALENT!!
DUE TO DIG MUDDLEY'S COLUMN THE MUSIC CRITICS CROWD HOLLYWOOD HALL—
SO WE'RE GOING TO HEAR THE WORLD'S MOST PERFECT PIANO-PLAYING— HERE? TONIGHT? HA!! HA!! HO!!
AFTER TONIGHT, DIG MUDDLEY WILL BE BACK MODELLING UNDERWEAR!!—
ELEVATOR TO THE CONCERT STAGE, MR - SIGH!!- LOVERBOYNIK?
AT THAT INSTANT—
CACKLE!!
SNIP!!
SO-AT THAT SAME INSTANT-
OOF!!
I'M TRAPPED!! HELP!!
4-29
MEANWHILE-
ROUND AN' ROUND!! CACKLE!! SNORT!!
AT THAT SAME INSTANT—
PIANO CONCERT TONITE HOLLYWOOD HALL
??-SUDDENLY, I'M DIZZY!! !!-WHERE AM I SUBBOSED TO BLAY TONIGHT?— ?? HOLLYWOOD HALL? THIS MUST BE THE BLACE!!-
AL CAPP
TO BE CONTINUED:

BEST COMICS IN THE WORLD

COMICS 19 · **Sunday Mirror** · **15¢**

NEW YORK, N. Y.   SUNDAY, MAY 6, 1956

LI'L ABNER by Al Capp

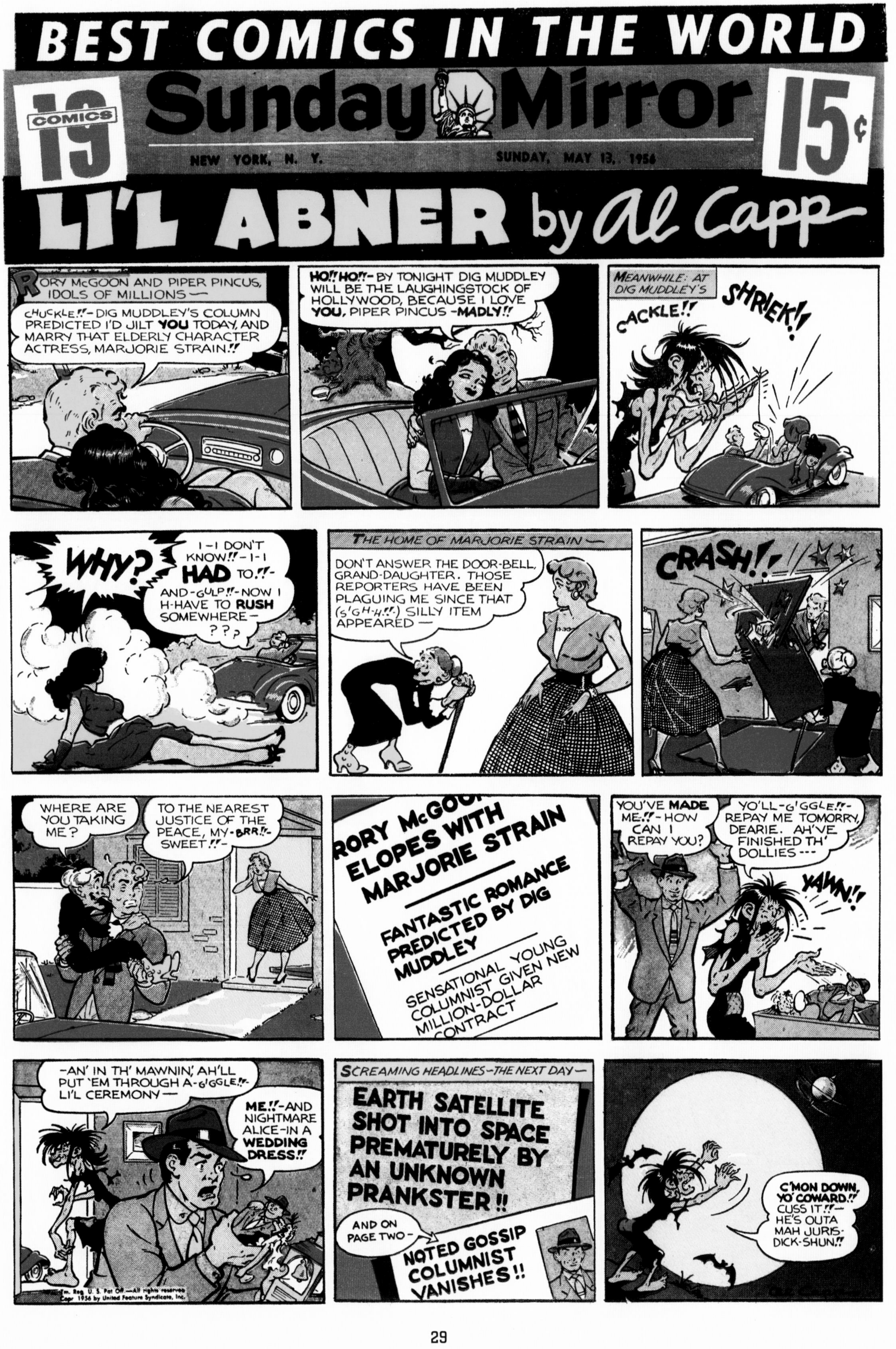
BEST COMICS IN THE WORLD
19 COMICS
Sunday Mirror
15¢
NEW YORK, N. Y.
SUNDAY, MAY 13, 1956
LI'L ABNER by Al Capp
RORY McGOON AND PIPER PINCUS, IDOLS OF MILLIONS —
CHUCKLE!! - DIG MUDDLEY'S COLUMN PREDICTED I'D JILT YOU TODAY, AND MARRY THAT ELDERLY CHARACTER ACTRESS, MARJORIE STRAIN!!
HO!! HO!! - BY TONIGHT DIG MUDDLEY WILL BE THE LAUGHINGSTOCK OF HOLLYWOOD, BECAUSE I LOVE YOU, PIPER PINCUS - MADLY!!
MEANWHILE: AT DIG MUDDLEY'S
CACKLE!!
SHRIEK!!
WHY?
I-I DON'T KNOW!! - I-I HAD TO.!! - AND - GULP!! - NOW I H-HAVE TO RUSH SOMEWHERE -
???
THE HOME OF MARJORIE STRAIN —
DON'T ANSWER THE DOOR-BELL, GRAND-DAUGHTER. THOSE REPORTERS HAVE BEEN PLAGUING ME SINCE THAT (S'GH-H!!) SILLY ITEM APPEARED —
CRASH!!
WHERE ARE YOU TAKING ME?
TO THE NEAREST JUSTICE OF THE PEACE, MY - BRR!! - SWEET!! -
RORY McGOON ELOPES WITH MARJORIE STRAIN
FANTASTIC ROMANCE PREDICTED BY DIG MUDDLEY
SENSATIONAL YOUNG COLUMNIST GIVEN NEW MILLION-DOLLAR CONTRACT
YOU'VE MADE ME!! - HOW CAN I REPAY YOU?
YO'LL - G'GGLE!! - REPAY ME TOMORRY, DEARIE. AH'VE FINISHED TH' DOLLIES ---
YAWN!!
-AN' IN TH' MAWNIN', AH'LL PUT 'EM THROUGH A - G'GGLE!! - LI'L CEREMONY —
ME!! - AND NIGHTMARE ALICE - IN A WEDDING DRESS!!
Tm. Reg. U. S. Pat Off — All rights reserved
Copr. 1956 by United Feature Syndicate, Inc.
SCREAMING HEADLINES - THE NEXT DAY —
EARTH SATELLITE SHOT INTO SPACE PREMATURELY BY AN UNKNOWN PRANKSTER!!
AND ON PAGE TWO -
NOTED GOSSIP COLUMNIST VANISHES!!
C'MON DOWN, YO' COWARD!! CUSS IT!! - HE'S OUTA MAH JURIS-DICK-SHUN!!

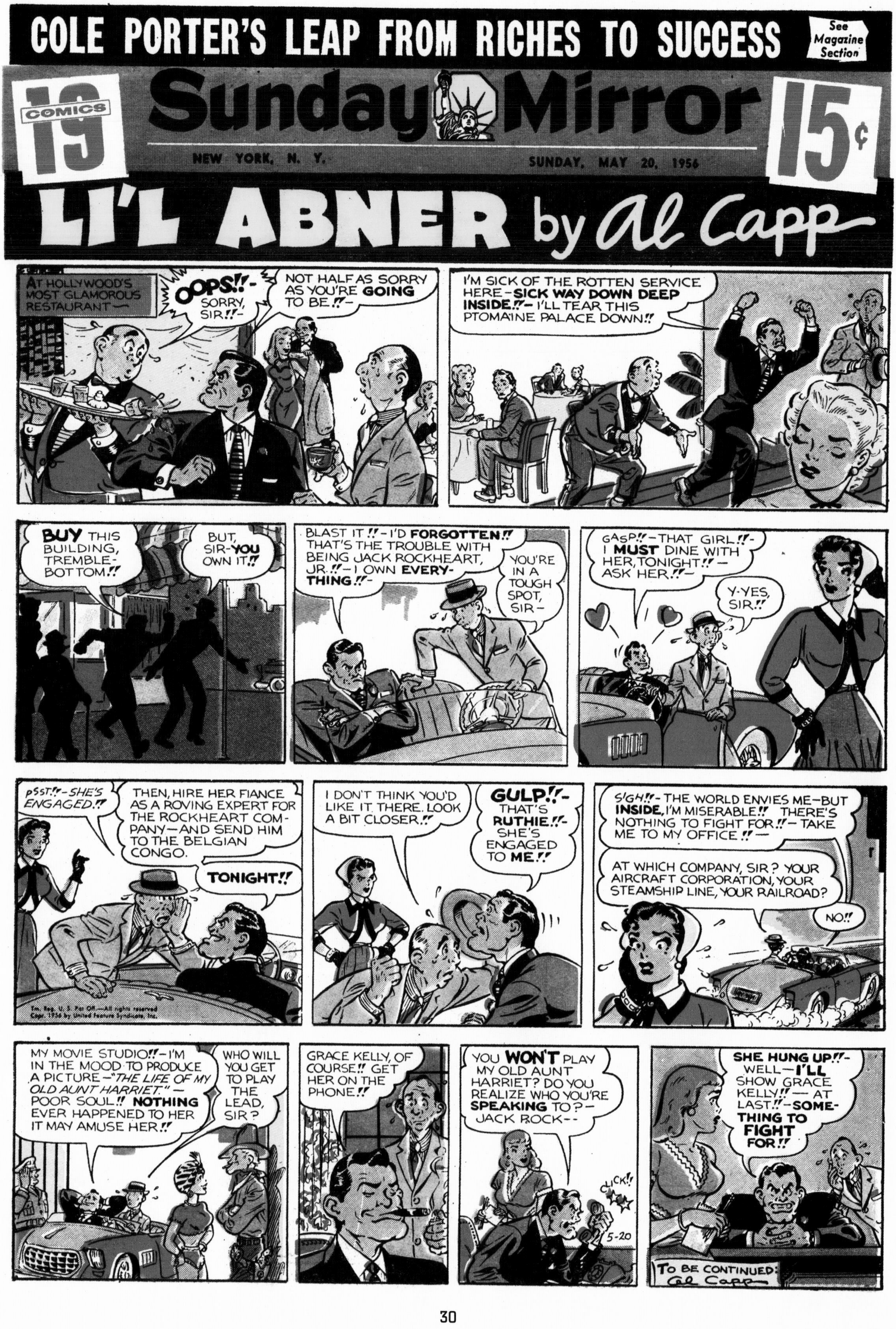

COLE PORTER'S LEAP FROM RICHES TO SUCCESS
See Magazine Section
19 COMICS
Sunday Mirror
15¢
NEW YORK, N. Y.
SUNDAY, MAY 20, 1956
LI'L ABNER by Al Capp
AT HOLLYWOOD'S MOST GLAMOROUS RESTAURANT —
OOPS!!- SORRY, SIR!!-
NOT HALF AS SORRY AS YOU'RE GOING TO BE!!-
I'M SICK OF THE ROTTEN SERVICE HERE-SICK WAY DOWN DEEP INSIDE!!- I'LL TEAR THIS PTOMAINE PALACE DOWN!!
BUY THIS BUILDING, TREMBLE-BOTTOM!!
BUT, SIR-YOU OWN IT!!
BLAST IT!!-I'D FORGOTTEN!! THAT'S THE TROUBLE WITH BEING JACK ROCKHEART, JR.!!-I OWN EVERY-THING!!-
YOU'RE IN A TOUGH SPOT, SIR-
GASP!!-THAT GIRL!!- I MUST DINE WITH HER, TONIGHT!!- ASK HER!!-
Y-YES, SIR!!
PSST!!-SHE'S ENGAGED!!
THEN, HIRE HER FIANCE AS A ROVING EXPERT FOR THE ROCKHEART COMPANY—AND SEND HIM TO THE BELGIAN CONGO.
TONIGHT!!
Tm. Reg. U. S. Pat. Off.—All rights reserved Copr. 1956 by United Feature Syndicate, Inc.
I DON'T THINK YOU'D LIKE IT THERE. LOOK A BIT CLOSER!!
GULP!!- THAT'S RUTHIE!!- SHE'S ENGAGED TO ME!!
SIGH!!-THE WORLD ENVIES ME-BUT INSIDE, I'M MISERABLE!! THERE'S NOTHING TO FIGHT FOR!!-TAKE ME TO MY OFFICE!!—
AT WHICH COMPANY, SIR? YOUR AIRCRAFT CORPORATION, YOUR STEAMSHIP LINE, YOUR RAILROAD?
NO!!
MY MOVIE STUDIO!!-I'M IN THE MOOD TO PRODUCE A PICTURE-"THE LIFE OF MY OLD AUNT HARRIET."- POOR SOUL!! NOTHING EVER HAPPENED TO HER IT MAY AMUSE HER!!
WHO WILL YOU GET TO PLAY THE LEAD, SIR?
GRACE KELLY, OF COURSE!! GET HER ON THE PHONE!!
YOU WON'T PLAY MY OLD AUNT HARRIET? DO YOU REALIZE WHO YOU'RE SPEAKING TO?- JACK ROCK--
CLICK!!
5-20
SHE HUNG UP!!- WELL-I'LL SHOW GRACE KELLY!!- AT LAST!!-SOME-THING TO FIGHT FOR!!
TO BE CONTINUED: Al Capp

LI'L ABNER

When better Grace Kellys are made, he'll make them!!

BY AL CAPP

19 COMICS
Sunday Mirror
15¢
NEW YORK, N. Y.
SUNDAY, JUNE 3, 1956

LI'L ABNER by Al Capp

19 COMICS Sunday Mirror 15¢

NEW YORK, N.Y.   SUNDAY, JUNE 10, 1956

LI'L ABNER by Al Capp

DAISY MAE FLIES TO HOLLYWOOD, ON THE TRANS-JACK-ROCKHEART JUNIOR-AIRLINES, LANDS AT JACK ROCK HEART JUNIOR FIELD, IS PUT UP AT THE HOTEL ROCKHEART-PLAZA, AND IS WHISKED TO THE ROCKHEART STUDIOS IN A ROCKHEART V-8.

INTRODUCING JACK ROCKHEART JUNIOR—**HIMSELF!!**

??—BUT YO' IS SORT OF A SHRIMP T'BE SECH A BIG MAN!!

SHE'S **BEAUTIFUL!!**—SHE'S **RADIANT!!**—SHE'S FORMED LIKE **VENUS!!**

WITH YOU—**WHO** NEEDS GRACE KELLY?

AND NOW TO FOLLOW EVERY STEP **SHE** TOOK UP THE LADDER TO THE STARS!!—HMM—LET'S SEE

RESEARCH REPORT

Subject: How Grace Kelly Made it

1. Was beautiful talented blonde, but unknown.
2. Given big chance with Bing Crosby in "The Country Girl." Won Academy Award
3. Was selected one of Best Dressed Women in the World.
4. Married Prince

WE'LL GIVE YOU A CHANCE WITH A **BIGGER** STAR THAN BING CROSBY!!—**BING CROSNIK, THE ORIGINAL!!** JUST IN FROM SLURVIA!! CROSBY LEARNED EVERY THING HE KNOWS FROM HIM!!—

IN MY GUNTRY IS NOPODY PIGGER THAN I AM!!

WE'LL GIVE YOU A **BETTER** STORY THAN "THE COUNTRY GIRL"!!—"**THE HUNGRY GIRL**"!!—IT'S THE GNAWING TALE OF A ONCE-GREAT MALE CORSET MODEL—

WHO BECAME A **HOPELESS FOOD ADDICT!!**—HE WON'T STOP EATING, WHILE HIS LOYAL WIFE STARVES!!—YOU **MUST** WIN THE ACADEMY AWARD FOR THE **REALISM** OF YOUR ACTING—

SO WE WON'T TAKE A **CHANCE** ON YOUR ACTING!! WE'LL **MAKE** IT REAL!!—YOU WON'T EAT **ANY**THING, WHILE WE SHOOT THE PICTURE. IT'LL TAKE **THREE MONTHS!!**

TH-THREE MONTHS?

6-10

DAISY MAE GETS ACADEMY AWARD, FOR "THE HUNGRY GIRL"

WINS OVER GRACE KELLY

ALSO NOSES OUT WALT, GENE, PATSY, PAUL, NANCY, EMMETT, AND SHIPWRECK KELLY.

Ceremony to be seen by entire nation tonight.

STOP BITING YOUR OSCAR!!

GULP!!—?? FO' A MINUTE AH THOUGHT IT WERE A CHOC'LIT SOLJER!!—

YOU MUST BE MIGHTY PROUD OF YOUR DISCOVERY TONIGHT—

SO FAR—SO GOOD!! NEXT STEP—"BEST DRESSED WOMAN." HA!!—WHO NEEDS GRACE KELLY?

Al Capp

TO BE CONTINUED

LI'L ABNER by Al Capp

HA!! WHO **NEEDS** GRACE KELLY? DAISY'S WON THE ACADEMY AWARD, SAME AS SHE DID!!— WHAT DID KELLY DO NEXT?

SHE WAS SELECTED "BEST-DRESSED WOMAN", SIR!!

THEN, **DAISY'LL** GRAB THE CROWN **THIS** YEAR!!" WHICH FASHION HOUSE DO WE OWN, TREMBLE-BOTTOM?

FATTIE FARTHINGALE'S, SIR.

GREAT!!— DOUBLE EVERYBODY'S SALARY THERE.— AND— HO!!—HO!!— WATCH THE PAPERS!!"

HAR!! HAR!!

ALL HIGH FASHION INDUSTRY ON STRIKE

"If everybody at Fattie Farthingale's can have their salaries doubled, why can't we?," roars spokesman.

FASHION EXECUTIVE PREDICTS STRIKE WON'T LAST LONG

"Sewing-machine girls are too poor to hold out!" he giggl...

JACK ROCKHE... JR., FAMOUS PHILAN-THROPIST, OFFERS TO PAY FULL WAGES TO STRIKERS, WHILE THEY REMAIN ON STRIKE !!

"So, why go back?" chuckles spokesman, on way to Riviera

ONLY FATTIE FARTHINGALE'S REMAINS OPEN !! But entire staff wor... ...own for mys...

BEST-DRESSED WOMAN TO BE SELECTED TONIGHT!!

I'M **SO** HUMILIATED!!— THIS RAG IS A WEEK OLD — BUT FATTIE FARTHINGALE CLAIMED SHE WAS TOO BUSY TO MAKE ME ANOTHER!!

I'M EMBARRASSED TO DEATH!!— I'VE ALREADY WORN THIS ONCE!!—BUT FATTIE FARTHINGALE REFUSED $10,000!!

L-LOOK!!—A **NEW** GOWN!!—

THE **WINNER!!**

GREAT!!— WE'VE FOLLOWED GRACE KELLY TO STEP NUMBER **TWO.!!**

HER **FINAL** TRIUMPH WAS MARRYING A PRINCE. ANY PRINCES AROUND FOR DAISY MAE?

FORTUNATELY, SIR — ONE ARRIVED TODAY!!— AND HE'S **SINGLE!!**

BONNIE PRINCE CHARLIE OF MONTE CARLOAD HERE, SEEKING BRIDE AND LOAN

Prince Charlie   Al Capp 6/17

BETWEEN US WE CAN HANDLE **BOTH** HIS NEEDS!!—

WE K-KIN?

34

19 COMICS Sunday Mirror 15¢

NEW YORK, N. Y. SUNDAY, JUNE 24, 1956

LI'L ABNER by Al Capp

THE STRANGE RIDDLE OF JOHN WAYNE
See Magazine Section
19 COMICS
Sunday Mirror
15¢
NEW YORK, N. Y.
SUNDAY, JULY 1, 1956
LI'L ABNER by Al Capp
ANY BABY-SITTIN' JOBS AVAILABLE, AVAILABLE?
JEST GOT A CALL FUM TH' CITY FOLKS AT TH' HUNTIN' LODGE. THEY WANTS A TALL, STRONG ONE —
TODAY'S MARRIAGE SPESHUL STRONG BUT SURLY. INTRODUCKSHUN $1.00 NON-REFUNDABLE.
PETS MINDED
AVAILABLE JONES. "I'll do anything for a price."
IS YORE LIFE UNBEARABLY HAPPY? AH'LL SEND MAH MOTHER-IN-LAW OVER 25¢ Per hour
AH'LL PHONE YO' IS ON YORE WAY —
LEMME CHECK MAH BABY-SETTIN' KIT. A CHANGE O' DIAPERS, TWO COMIC BOOKS, A RATTLE, A HAM SANGWIDGE FO' ME, AN' A LI'L HAM BONE FO' TH' BABY. AH IS ALL SET.
AH IS TH' TALL, STRONG ONE — AS ANY FOOL KIN PLAINLY SEE. SEE?
COME IN. I'M THE BABY. THEY -GIGGLE!!- SENT JUST WHAT I ORDERED.
GULP!! — HAIN'T NOTHIN' SUITABLE IN THIS KIT. UH — WOULD YO' LIKE TO PLAY SOME SORT O' GAME?
LET'S PLAY "GUESS WHO"!!
NOW, WHAT HAPPENS?
GASP!!
GUESS WHO?
YO'!!
RIGHT!! YOU WIN!! NOW, IT'S MY TURN.
CHUCKLE!!
GUESS WHO —
YOU!!
WRONG. HIM!!
YOU'RE AN IDIOT!!
NATCHERLY. AH IS ONLY 15½ Y'ARS OLD!!
YOU'RE ENTIRELY TOO YOUNG FOR ME!!
YAS'M. H-HOW OLD IS YO'?
15½
??— M-MAMMY? — HAIN'T A 15½-Y'AR-OLE BOY JEST AS OLD AS A 15½-Y'AR-OLE GAL?
WRONG.
15½-Y'AR-OLE GALS IS MUCH OLDER!!
THASS ONE O' WHUT THEY CALLS TH' FACTS O' LIFE, SON!! —
Tm. Reg. U. S. Pat. Off.—All rights reserved Copr. 1956 by United Feature Syndicate, Inc.
7-1 Al Capp

COMICS 19 **Sunday Mirror** **15¢**

NEW YORK, N. Y.   SUNDAY, JULY 8, 1956

LI'L ABNER by Al Capp

37

COMICS 19 · **Sunday Mirror** · **15¢**

NEW YORK, N. Y.   SUNDAY, JULY 15, 1954

LI'L ABNER by Al Capp

COMICS 19   Sunday Mirror   15¢

NEW YORK, N. Y.   SUNDAY, JULY 22, 1956

LI'L ABNER by Al Capp

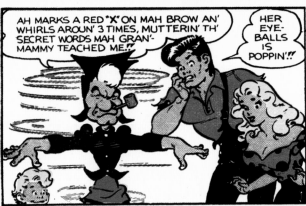

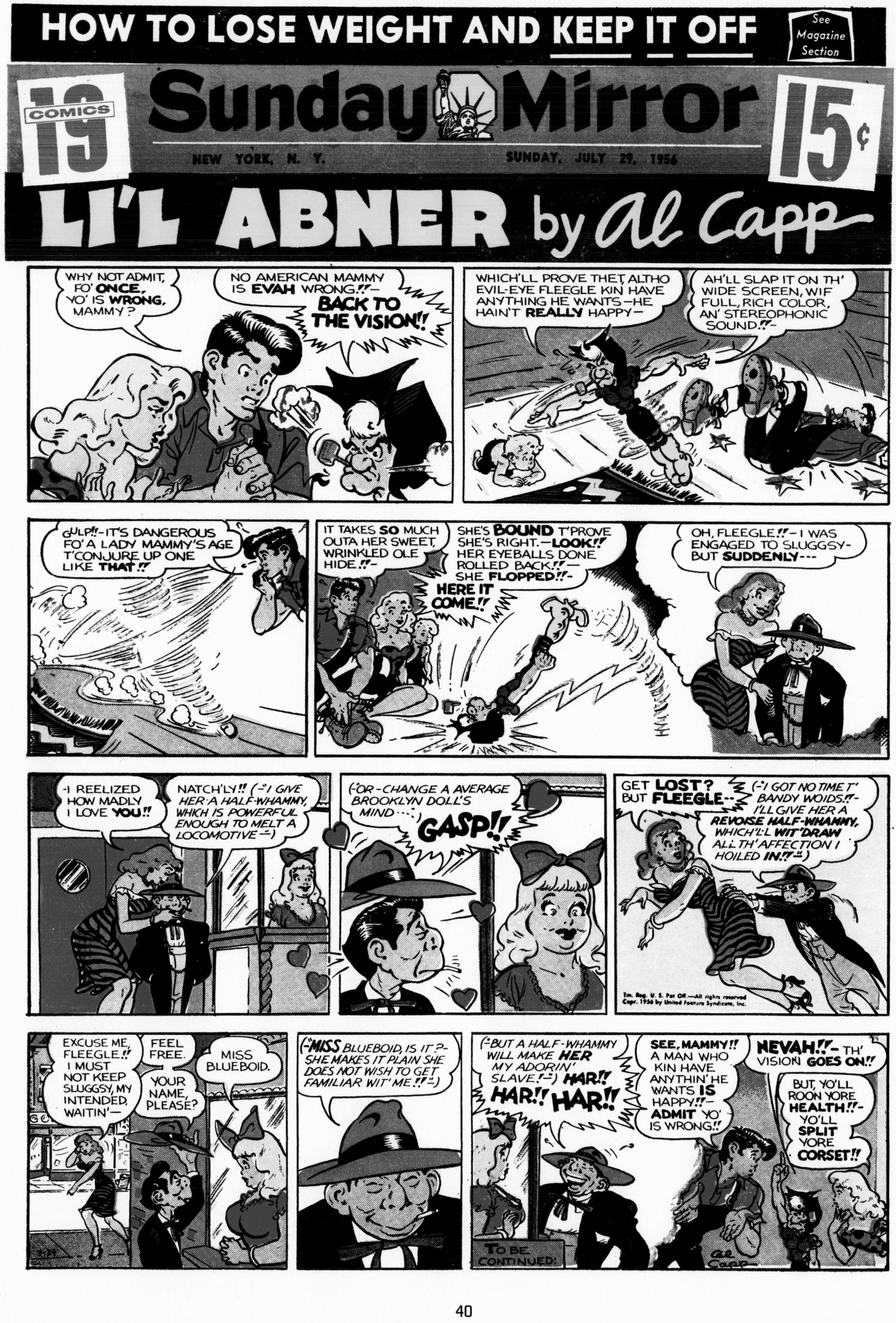
HOW TO LOSE WEIGHT AND KEEP IT OFF
See Magazine Section
19 COMICS
Sunday Mirror
15¢
NEW YORK, N. Y.
SUNDAY, JULY 29, 1956
LI'L ABNER by Al Capp
WHY NOT ADMIT, FO' ONCE, YO' IS WRONG, MAMMY?
NO AMERICAN MAMMY IS EVAH WRONG!!–
BACK TO THE VISION!!
WHICH'LL PROVE THET, ALTHO EVIL-EYE FLEEGLE KIN HAVE ANYTHING HE WANTS—HE HAIN'T REALLY HAPPY—
AH'LL SLAP IT ON TH' WIDE SCREEN, WIF FULL, RICH COLOR, AN' STEREOPHONIC SOUND!!–
GULP!!–IT'S DANGEROUS FO' A LADY MAMMY'S AGE T'CONJURE UP ONE LIKE THAT!!
IT TAKES SO MUCH OUTA HER SWEET, WRINKLED OLE HIDE!!–
SHE'S BOUND T'PROVE SHE'S RIGHT.—LOOK!! HER EYEBALLS DONE ROLLED BACK!!—SHE FLOPPED!!–
HERE IT COME!!
OH, FLEEGLE!!–I WAS ENGAGED TO SLUGGSY-BUT SUDDENLY---
-I REELIZED HOW MADLY I LOVE YOU!!
NATCH'LY!! (–I GIVE HER A HALF-WHAMMY, WHICH IS POWERFUL ENOUGH TO MELT A LOCOMOTIVE–)
(–OR-CHANGE A AVERAGE BROOKLYN DOLL'S MIND–)
GASP!!
GET LOST? BUT FLEEGLE--
(–I GOT NO TIME T' BANDY WOIDS!!–I'LL GIVE HER A REVOISE HALF-WHAMMY, WHICH'LL WIT'DRAW ALL TH' AFFECTION I HOILED IN!!–)
Tm. Reg. U. S. Pat. Off.—All rights reserved Copr. 1956 by United Feature Syndicate, Inc.
EXCUSE ME, FLEEGLE!! I MUST NOT KEEP SLUGGSY, MY INTENDED, WAITIN'—
FEEL FREE.
YOUR NAME, PLEASE?
MISS BLUEBOID.
(–MISS BLUEBOID, IS IT?–SHE MAKES IT PLAIN SHE DOES NOT WISH TO GET FAMILIAR WIT' ME!!–)
(–BUT A HALF-WHAMMY WILL MAKE HER MY ADORIN' SLAVE!–) HAR!! HAR!! HAR!!
SEE, MAMMY!! A MAN WHO KIN HAVE ANYTHIN' HE WANTS IS HAPPY!!–ADMIT YO' IS WRONG!!
NEVAH!!–TH' VISION GOES ON!!
BUT, YO'LL ROON YORE HEALTH!!–YO'LL SPLIT YORE CORSET!!
TO BE CONTINUED!
AL CAPP

19 COMICS

Sunday Mirror

15¢

NEW YORK, N. Y.   SUNDAY, AUGUST 5, 1956

LI'L ABNER by Al Capp

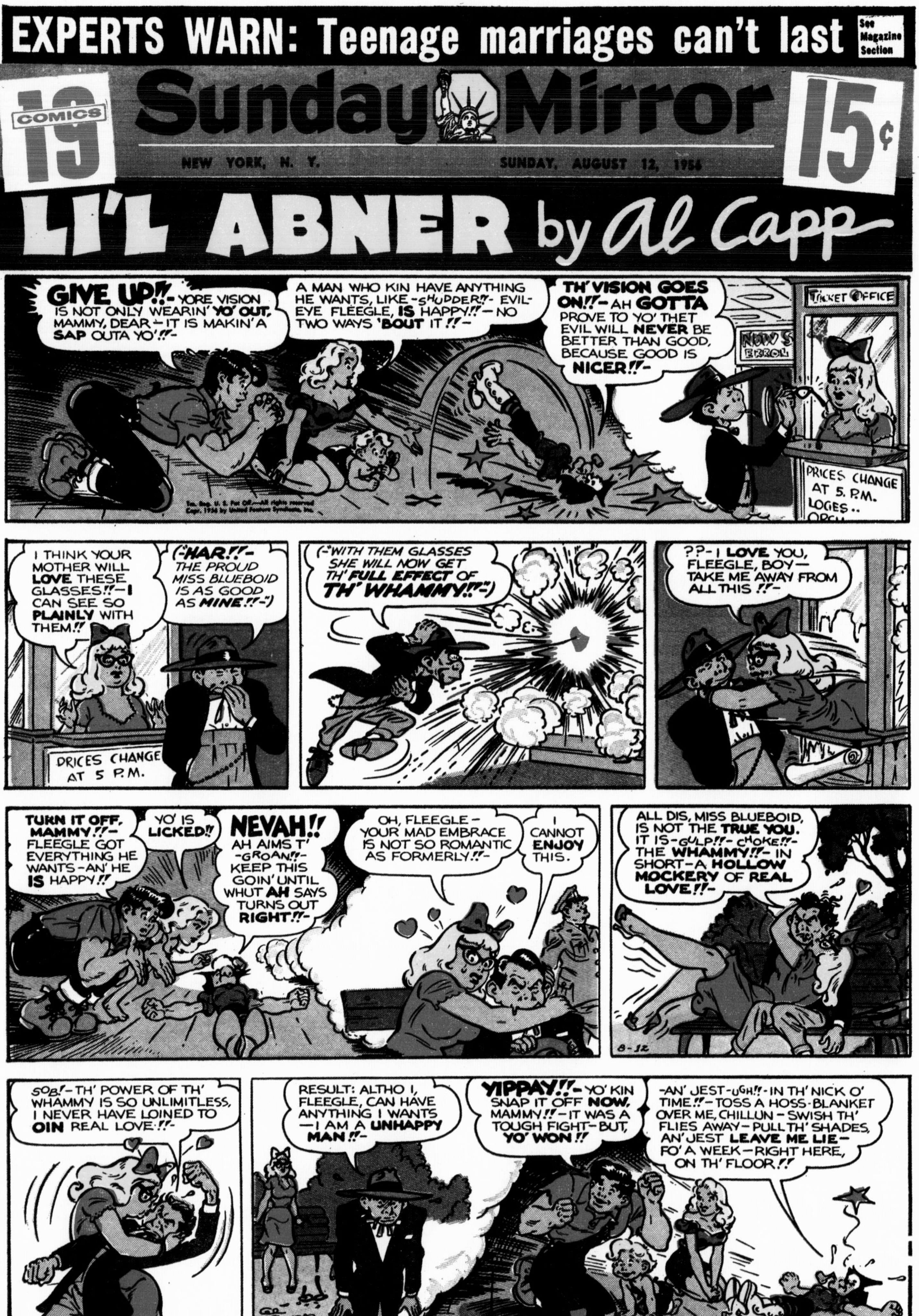
EXPERTS WARN: Teenage marriages can't last
See Magazine Section
19 COMICS
Sunday Mirror
15¢
NEW YORK, N. Y.
SUNDAY, AUGUST 12, 1956
LI'L ABNER by Al Capp
GIVE UP!!—YORE VISION IS NOT ONLY WEARIN' YO' OUT, MAMMY, DEAR—IT IS MAKIN' A SAP OUTA YO'!!—
A MAN WHO KIN HAVE ANYTHING HE WANTS, LIKE—SHUDDER!!—EVIL-EYE FLEEGLE, IS HAPPY!!—NO TWO WAYS 'BOUT IT!!—
TH' VISION GOES ON!!—AH GOTTA PROVE TO YO' THET EVIL WILL NEVER BE BETTER THAN GOOD, BECAUSE GOOD IS NICER!!—
TICKET OFFICE
PRICES CHANGE AT 5. P.M. LOGES..
I THINK YOUR MOTHER WILL LOVE THESE GLASSES!!—I CAN SEE SO PLAINLY WITH THEM!!
(—HAR!!—THE PROUD MISS BLUEBOID IS AS GOOD AS MINE!!—)
PRICES CHANGE AT 5 P.M.
(—WITH THEM GLASSES SHE WILL NOW GET TH' FULL EFFECT OF TH' WHAMMY!!—)
??—I LOVE YOU, FLEEGLE, BOY—TAKE ME AWAY FROM ALL THIS!!—
TURN IT OFF, MAMMY!!—FLEEGLE GOT EVERYTHING HE WANTS—AN' HE IS HAPPY!!
YO' IS LICKED!!
NEVAH!! AH AIMS T' —GROAN!!—KEEP THIS GOIN' UNTIL WHUT AH SAYS TURNS OUT RIGHT!!—
OH, FLEEGLE—YOUR MAD EMBRACE IS NOT SO ROMANTIC AS FORMERLY!!—
I CANNOT ENJOY THIS.
ALL DIS, MISS BLUEBOID, IS NOT THE TRUE YOU. IT IS—GULP!!—CHOKE!!—THE WHAMMY!!—IN SHORT—A HOLLOW MOCKERY OF REAL LOVE!!—
8-12
SOB!—TH' POWER OF TH' WHAMMY IS SO UNLIMITLESS, I NEVER HAVE LOINED TO OIN REAL LOVE!!—
RESULT: ALTHO I, FLEEGLE, CAN HAVE ANYTHING I WANTS—I AM A UNHAPPY MAN!!—
YIPPAY!!—YO' KIN SNAP IT OFF NOW, MAMMY!!—IT WAS A TOUGH FIGHT—BUT, YO' WON!!
—AN' JEST—UGH!!—IN TH' NICK O' TIME!!—TOSS A HOSS-BLANKET OVER ME, CHILLUN—SWISH TH' FLIES AWAY—PULL TH' SHADES, AN' JEST LEAVE ME LIE—FO' A WEEK—RIGHT HERE, ON TH' FLOOR!!
Al Capp

THE DANCE OF A LIFETIME

See Magazine Section

18 COMICS

Sunday Mirror

15¢

NEW YORK, N. Y.

SUNDAY, AUGUST 19, 1956

LI'L ABNER by Al Capp

RECKON WE'S TH' HAPPIEST FAMBLY IN ALL CREATION!!—LOTS O' FOOD, NOT MUCH WORK—AN' EV'RYBODY HAPPY AS HAWGS!!

NO CROPS T' WORRY 'BOUT, BECUZ WE DIDN'T PLANT ANY!!

NO MONEY T' LOSE, BECUZ WE HAIN'T GOT ANY!!

OWOOOOO!!

THAR IT GO AGIN!!—THET M-MOURNFUL SOUND.!!

SEEMS T'COME FUM BELOW!!

N-NO!! IT'S COMIN' FUM ABOVE!!

IF YO' AX ME—IT'S COMIN' FUM ALL AROUND US!!

SHECKS!!—IT DON'T MEAN NOTHIN'!! IT JEST SOUNDS AS THOUGH DOOMSDAY WAS APPROACHIN'—

PANSY!! GUESS WHO'S APPROACHIN'!!

YORE ONCLE PEARLY G. YOKUM!! ??—WHUT'S TH' "G" STAND FO'?

NO TIME FO' CHIT-CHAT!! GRAB TH' CHILE, DAISY MAE, AN' LET'S HEAD FO' TH' HILLS!!

NO SENSE PANICKIN'!! IF PEARLY G. YOKUM IS COMIN' T' SEE US—HE'LL FIND US!!

WHAR YO' GOIN', MAMMY?

WE GOT JEST ONE CHANCE.!!

AH IS GONNA MEET HIM BEFO' HE GITS HERE—AN' HEAD HIM OFF!!

THET "G"! WHUT DO IT STAND FO'?

IT'S B-BETTER NOT TO KNOW!!

(="THAR HE IS!!—FAT AN' CHEERFUL AS A CLAM!! LI'L DO HE REELIZE HOW HIS APPROACH STRIKES TERROR INTO INNERCENT HEARTS!!"=)

HOWDY, PANSY!! AH JEST HAD A HANKERIN' T' VISIT YO'!!

WHY VISIT US? TH' FOOD HAIN'T GOOD!!—OUR COMPANY IS BORIN'—

—AN' OUR NEIGHBORS IS UNSANITARY, AN' QUARRELSOME—

AH JEST HAPPENS T' HAVE OUR LIFE-SAVIN'S WIF ME. TAKE IT!!—GO VISIT SOME NICE PLACE. LOOIEVILLE, KAINTUCKY!! MONTE CARLO!!—TH' GRAND CANYON—

THEM—SIGH!!—SHORE IS NICE PLACES, PANSY—AN' AH'D SHORE LIKE TO VISIT 'EM—SOMETIME.

8-19

BUT, RIGHT NOW—AH GOT A POW'FUL HANKERIN' T' VISIT YO'!!!

H-HAS YO', PEARLY G. YOKUM?

Al Capp

WHY IS PEARLY G. YOKUM SO UNWELCOME? WHAT DOES THE "G" STAND FOR?

43

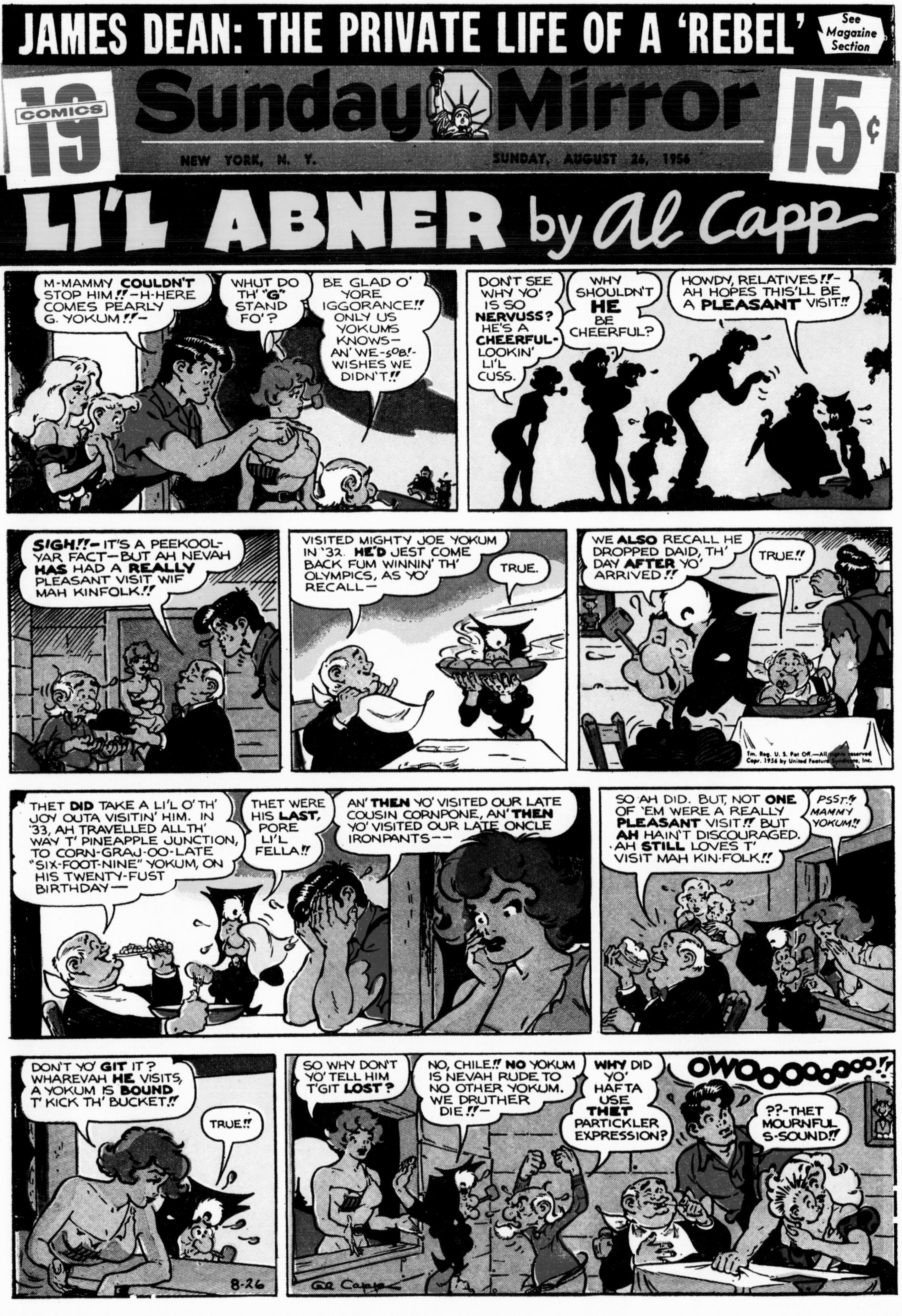
JAMES DEAN: THE PRIVATE LIFE OF A 'REBEL'
See Magazine Section
19 COMICS
Sunday Mirror
15¢
NEW YORK, N. Y.
SUNDAY, AUGUST 26, 1956
LI'L ABNER by Al Capp
M-MAMMY COULDN'T STOP HIM!!–H-HERE COMES PEARLY G. YOKUM!!–
WHUT DO TH' "G" STAND FO'?
BE GLAD O' YORE IGGORANCE!! ONLY US YOKUMS KNOWS– AN' WE-SOB!-WISHES WE DIDN'T!!
DON'T SEE WHY YO' IS SO NERVUSS? HE'S A CHEERFUL-LOOKIN' LI'L CUSS.
WHY SHOULDN'T HE BE CHEERFUL?
HOWDY, RELATIVES!!– AH HOPES THIS'LL BE A PLEASANT VISIT!!
SIGH!!– IT'S A PEEKOOL-YAR FACT–BUT AH NEVAH HAS HAD A REALLY PLEASANT VISIT WIF MAH KINFOLK!!
VISITED MIGHTY JOE YOKUM IN '32. HE'D JEST COME BACK FUM WINNIN' TH' OLYMPICS, AS YO' RECALL–
TRUE.
WE ALSO RECALL HE DROPPED DAID, TH' DAY AFTER YO' ARRIVED!!
TRUE!!
Tm. Reg. U. S. Pat Off.—All rights reserved Copr. 1956 by United Feature Syndicate, Inc.
THET DID TAKE A LI'L O'TH' JOY OUTA VISITIN' HIM. IN '33, AH TRAVELLED ALL TH' WAY T' PINEAPPLE JUNCTION, TO CORN-GRAJ-OO-LATE "SIX-FOOT-NINE" YOKUM, ON HIS TWENTY-FUST BIRTHDAY–
THET WERE HIS LAST, PORE LI'L FELLA!!
AN' THEN YO' VISITED OUR LATE COUSIN CORNPONE, AN' THEN YO' VISITED OUR LATE ONCLE IRONPANTS––
SO AH DID. BUT, NOT ONE OF 'EM WERE A REALLY PLEASANT VISIT!! BUT AH HAIN'T DISCOURAGED. AH STILL LOVES T' VISIT MAH KIN-FOLK!!
PSST!! MAMMY YOKUM!!
DON'T YO' GIT IT? WHAREVAH HE VISITS, A YOKUM IS BOUND T' KICK TH' BUCKET!!
TRUE!!
8-26
SO WHY DON'T YO' TELL HIM T'GIT LOST?
NO, CHILE!! NO YOKUM IS NEVAH RUDE TO NO OTHER YOKUM. WE DRUTHER DIE!!–
WHY DID YO' HAFTA USE THET PARTICKLER EXPRESSION?
OWOOOOOOOO!!
??–THET MOURNFUL S-SOUND!!
Al Capp

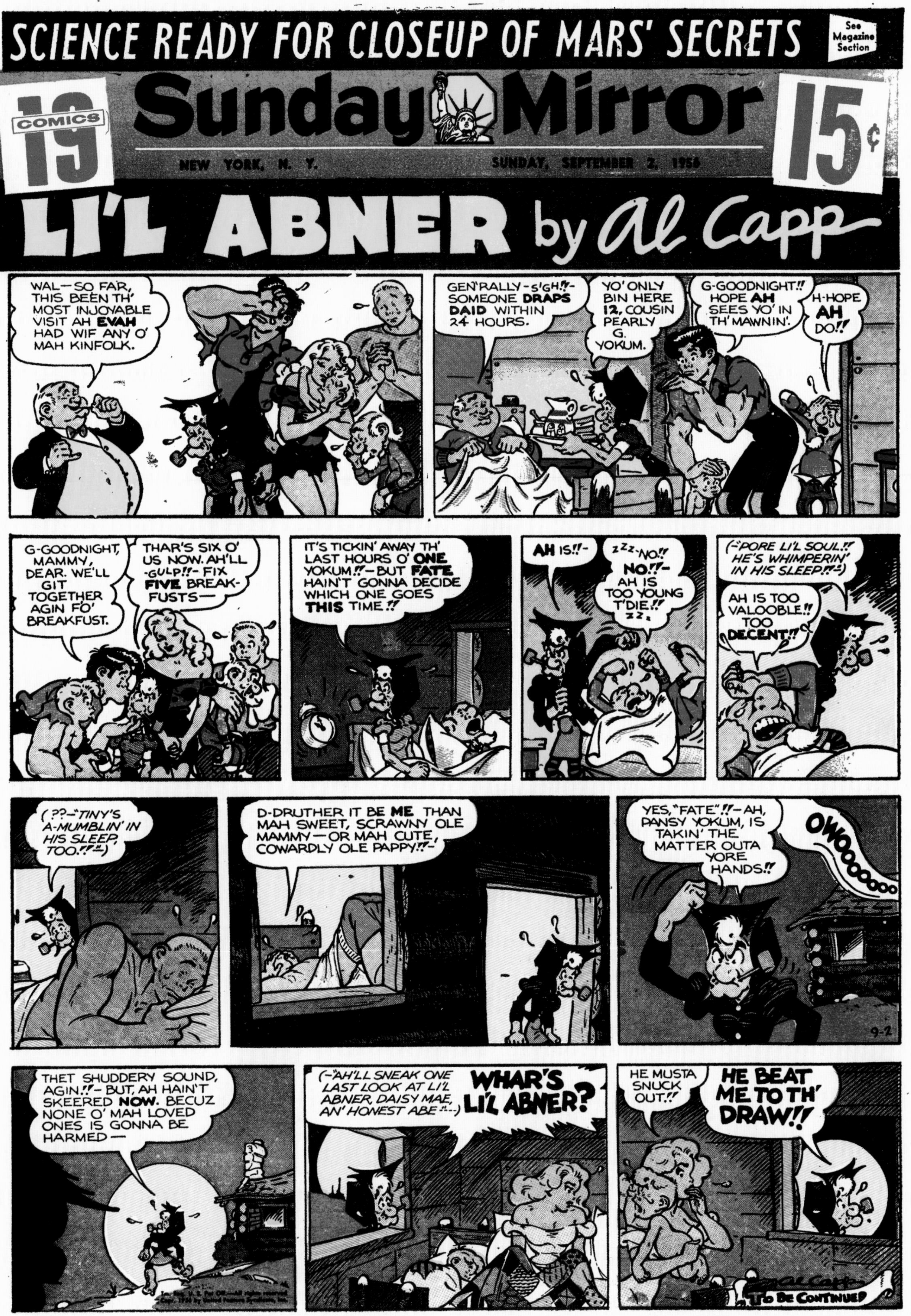
SCIENCE READY FOR CLOSEUP OF MARS' SECRETS
See Magazine Section
COMICS 19
Sunday Mirror
15¢
NEW YORK, N. Y.
SUNDAY, SEPTEMBER 2, 1956
LI'L ABNER by Al Capp
WAL—SO FAR, THIS BEEN TH' MOST INJOYABLE VISIT AH EVAH HAD WIF ANY O' MAH KINFOLK.
GEN'RALLY-SIGH!!-SOMEONE DRAPS DAID WITHIN 24 HOURS.
YO' ONLY BIN HERE 12, COUSIN PEARLY G. YOKUM.
G-GOODNIGHT!! HOPE AH SEES YO' IN TH' MAWNIN'.
H-HOPE AH DO!!
G-GOODNIGHT, MAMMY, DEAR. WE'LL GIT TOGETHER AGIN FO' BREAKFUST.
THAR'S SIX O' US NOW. AH'LL -GULP!!- FIX FIVE BREAKFUSTS—
IT'S TICKIN' AWAY TH' LAST HOURS O' ONE YOKUM!!—BUT FATE HAIN'T GONNA DECIDE WHICH ONE GOES THIS TIME!!
AH IS!!-
ZZZ-NO!! NO!!- AH IS TOO YOUNG T'DIE!! ZZZ
(-PORE LI'L SOUL!! HE'S WHIMPERIN' IN HIS SLEEP!!-)
AH IS TOO VALOOBLE!! TOO DECENT!!
(??-TINY'S A-MUMBLIN' IN HIS SLEEP, TOO.!!-)
D-DRUTHER IT BE ME THAN MAH SWEET, SCRAWNY OLE MAMMY—OR MAH CUTE, COWARDLY OLE PAPPY!!-
YES, "FATE"!!—AH, PANSY YOKUM, IS TAKIN' THE MATTER OUTA YORE HANDS!!
OWOOOOOOOO
9-2
THET SHUDDERY SOUND, AGIN!!—BUT, AH HAIN'T SKEERED NOW. BECUZ NONE O' MAH LOVED ONES IS GONNA BE HARMED—
(-AH'LL SNEAK ONE LAST LOOK AT LI'L ABNER, DAISY MAE, AN' HONEST ABE-)
WHAR'S LI'L ABNER?
HE MUSTA SNUCK OUT!!
HE BEAT ME TO TH' DRAW!!
AL CAPP
TO BE CONTINUED

Sunday Mirror

COMICS **19**   **15¢**

NEW YORK, N. Y.   SUNDAY, SEPTEMBER 9, 1956

LI'L ABNER by Al Capp

ONCLE PEARLY G. YOKUM ARRIVED, 12 HOURS AGO. WITHIN TH' **NEXT** 12 HOURS —A YOKUM IS **BOUND T'DIE!!**

AH DECIDED IT BETTER BE **ME!!** BUT LI'L ABNER BEAT ME TO TH' DRAW!!

??—HIS FOOTPRINTS, GOIN' **UP** CORNPONE'S LEAP!!

HE GOT A START ON ME TO TH' **TOP**—BUT, MEBBE AH KIN BEAT HIM TO **TH' BOTTOM!!**

AH MUST BE IN HEVVIN—ON ACCOUNT AH SEES A ANGEL'S FACE!!

THASS MIGHTY SWEET O' YO', SON, BUT IT'S MERELY YORE SCRAWNY OLE MAMMY!!

LUCKY YO' HAIN'T AS HEAVY AS TINY, OR AH'D OF BIN DRIV **CLEAR OUTA SIGHT!!**

YO' **KETCHED** ME, LI'L ABNER!!

WRONG!!—MAMMY KETCHED US **BOTH!!**

??—AH DON'T SEE HER!!

HERE AH IS!!—REACH DOWN, AN' YANK ME UP!!

9-9 Tm. Reg. U. S. Pat Off.—All rights reserved — Copr. 1956 by United Feature Syndicate, Inc.

SO FAR, **THREE** YOKUMS HAS TRIED T' SACK-REE-FICE THEMSELFS T' SATISFY FATE!!—

THAR'S JEST ONE YOKUM LEFT— **PAPPY!!**

NO DOUBT, **HE'LL** BE ZOOMIN' OFFA THET CLIFF ANY MINUTE NOW, PORE BRAVE LI'L SOUL— IN A EFFORT T'SAVE **US!!**—

BOYS !!— GIT INTO PO-ZISHUN T' KETCH BRAVE LI'L PAPPY!!

MAMMY!!—AH BIN IN THIS PO-ZISHUN NINE HOURS, AN' NO BRAVE LI'L PAPPY!!

GULP!! MEBBE FATE DONE TRICKED US!!—MEBBE FATE NAILED HIM WHILE HE SLEPT AT HOME!!

OWOOOOOOOO THET'S COMIN' FUM **OUR** HOUSE!!

TO BE CONTINUED :

46

Sunday Mirror

18 COMICS   NEW YORK, N. Y.   SUNDAY, SEPTEMBER 16, 1956   15¢

LI'L ABNER by Al Capp

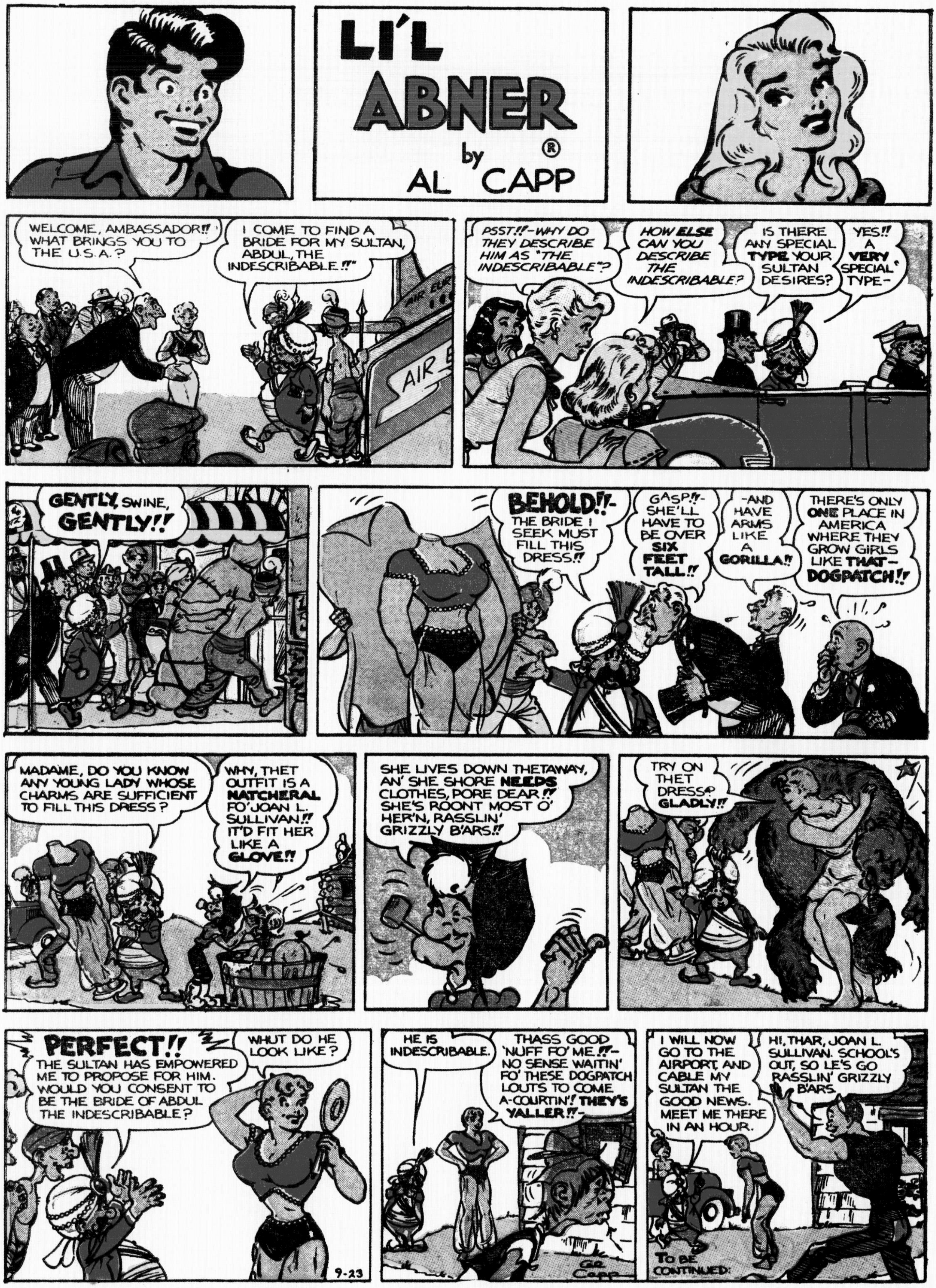
LI'L ABNER
by AL CAPP ®
WELCOME, AMBASSADOR!! WHAT BRINGS YOU TO THE U.S.A.?
I COME TO FIND A BRIDE FOR MY SULTAN, ABDUL, THE INDESCRIBABLE!!"
PSST!!-WHY DO THEY DESCRIBE HIM AS "THE INDESCRIBABLE"?
HOW ELSE CAN YOU DESCRIBE THE INDESCRIBABLE?
IS THERE ANY SPECIAL TYPE YOUR SULTAN DESIRES?
YES!! A VERY SPECIAL TYPE-
GENTLY, SWINE, GENTLY!!
BEHOLD!!- THE BRIDE I SEEK MUST FILL THIS DRESS!!
GASP!!- SHE'LL HAVE TO BE OVER SIX FEET TALL!!
-AND HAVE ARMS LIKE A GORILLA!!
THERE'S ONLY ONE PLACE IN AMERICA WHERE THEY GROW GIRLS LIKE THAT- DOGPATCH!!
MADAME, DO YOU KNOW ANY YOUNG LADY WHOSE CHARMS ARE SUFFICIENT TO FILL THIS DRESS?
WHY, THET OUTFIT IS A NATCHERAL FO' JOAN L. SULLIVAN!! IT'D FIT HER LIKE A GLOVE!!
SHE LIVES DOWN THETAWAY, AN' SHE SHORE NEEDS CLOTHES, PORE DEAR!! SHE'S ROONT MOST O' HER'N, RASSLIN' GRIZZLY B'ARS!!
TRY ON THET DRESS?
GLADLY!!
PERFECT!!
THE SULTAN HAS EMPOWERED ME TO PROPOSE FOR HIM. WOULD YOU CONSENT TO BE THE BRIDE OF ABDUL THE INDESCRIBABLE?
WHUT DO HE LOOK LIKE?
9-23
HE IS INDESCRIBABLE.
THASS GOOD 'NUFF FO' ME.!!- NO SENSE WAITIN' FO' THESE DOGPATCH LOUTS TO COME A-COURTIN'! THEY'S YALLER!!-
Al Capp
I WILL NOW GO TO THE AIRPORT AND CABLE MY SULTAN THE GOOD NEWS. MEET ME THERE IN AN HOUR.
HI, THAR, JOAN L. SULLIVAN. SCHOOL'S OUT, SO LE'S GO RASSLIN' GRIZZLY B'ARS.
TO BE CONTINUED.

Geography, 4th Grade   Page 17

ABDUL THE INDESCRIBABLE

Absolute ruler of 10,000,000. Although an enlightened monarch, he still maintains the ancient tradition of marrying 100 girls every year, from 100 different nations---to encourage international brotherhood.

There is no available photograph, portrait or description of Abdul the Indescribable.

TO BE CONTINUED!

Sunday Mirror 15¢

19 COMICS

NEW YORK, N. Y.   SUNDAY, OCTOBER 7, 1956

LI'L ABNER *by Al Capp*

50

Sunday Mirror 15¢

NEW YORK, N. Y.   SUNDAY, OCTOBER 14, 1956

LI'L ABNER by Al Capp

BEHOLD!! — OH LUCKY 100 BRIDES-TO-BE!! HERE COMES YOUR HUSBAND-TO-BE, **ABDUL THE INDESCRIBABLE** — IN ALL HIS DAZZLING SPLENDOR.!!

PORE SOUL!!

SH!!—NO ONE IS SUPPOSED TO NOTICE THERE IS ANYTHING ODD ABOUT HIM!!

SHECKS.!!—THAR **HAIN'T** NOTHIN' ODD 'BOUT HIM!!

HE GOT "CURVATURE O' TH' SWINE." THASS COMMON AMONGST PIGS, IN DOGPATCH!!

AH KIN FIX IT, EASY!!— AH DONE IT, **MILLYUNS** O' TIMES.!!

SNAP!!

OH, LOVELY FLOWER FROM SAVAGE AMERICA.!!—OUT OF GRATITUDE, I WILL GRANT YOU YOUR DEAREST WISH.!!

NATURALLY, IT WOULD BE THAT I SEND HOME THE OTHER 99, AND MARRY YOU!!

CONTRARIWISE.!! MARRY **T'OTHER** 99 —AN' SEND **ME** HOME.!!—

10-14

WHAR YO' BIN, FO' TH' LAST COUPLE O' WEEKS?

AH ALMOST GOT MARRIED!!

WAL, DON'T LET TH' DISAPPOINTMENT BREAK YORE HEART, SON. AT 15½, IT COULDN'T O' BIN MORE'N A CHILDISH CRUSH.!!

Sunday Mirror

18 COMICS

15¢

NEW YORK, N. Y.

SUNDAY, OCTOBER 21, 1956

LI'L ABNER by Al Capp

THE BLEARY HABITUÉS OF NEW YORK'S SEEDIEST NIGHT CLUB ARE **ELECTRIFIED** BY THE SAVAGE, DANCING BEAUTY OF **BAGMAR!!**

WHEEOO!!

WOW!!

YOWEE!!

BUT—ONE FACE IN THAT LOW CROWD HAS A CERTAIN CRAGGY NOBILITY. THAT GRANITE CHIN, THAT CLARET-COLORED NOSE, THAT CIGAR——-???!!—

YES!!— IT'S A TWO-DOLLAR CIGAR.!!

THIS IS A MAN TO BE RECKONED WITH!!

THE PERFORMANCE OVER—TWO NOBLE FIGURES DEPART—BAGMAR TO HER DRESSING ROOM, AND---

GOT A NICKEL, MISTER?

OF **COURSE**, I'VE GOT A NICKEL.!!

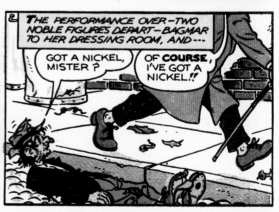

GENERAL BULLMOOSE, SIR!!—THANK HEAVENS YOU'VE RETURNED, SAFELY, FROM YOUR SLUMMING TRIP!!

(—"BY CHARLIE WILSON!!" THAT BAGMAR HAUNTS ME!!" WHAT SPLENDID CONDITION SHE'S IN!!"—WHAT A PROFOUND STUDENT OF THE DANCE!!")

(—"I'D LIKE TO KNOW THAT YOUNG LADY BETTER.!!"—BUT, FOR GENERAL BULLMOOSE TO PUBLICLY CALL UPON A PERFORMER IN **SUCH** A JOINT—WOULD CAUSE A PANIC ON WALL STREET!!"—)

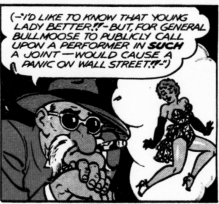

(—"I **COULD** SEE HER SECRETLY— BUT, HOW THEN COULD I TELL IF IT WAS MY MILLIONS SHE ADMIRED—INSTEAD OF SIMPLE, ROMANTIC ME.!!"")

(—"BY JOHN BRICKER!!"—I HAVE IT!!"—) **SQUIRMINGHAM!!**— FIND ME THE WORLD'S GREATEST MAKE-UP EXPERT, AND ANY CHEAP CHARACTER ACTOR MY **SIZE**.!!

YES, SIR!!

CAN YOU MAKE **HIM** LOOK LIKE ME—AND **ME** LIKE **HIM**?—

GIVE ME AN HOUR—

10·21

ONE HOUR LATER—

BY **CONRAD HILTON**!! YOU LOOK HANDSOME.!!— **COMMANDING.!!**—DEBONAIR!!— IN OTHER WORDS—YOU LOOK LIKE **ME**.!!—MY OWN BODYGUARDS WOULD TAKE ORDERS FROM **YOU**—

ER— DO YOU THINK THEY **WOULD**, SIR?

TO BE CONTINUED.

Sunday Mirror 15¢

NEW YORK, N. Y.   SUNDAY, OCTOBER 28, 1956

LI'L ABNER by Al Capp

Sunday Mirror

NEW YORK, N. Y.   SUNDAY, NOVEMBER 4, 1956   15¢

LI'L ABNER by Al Capp

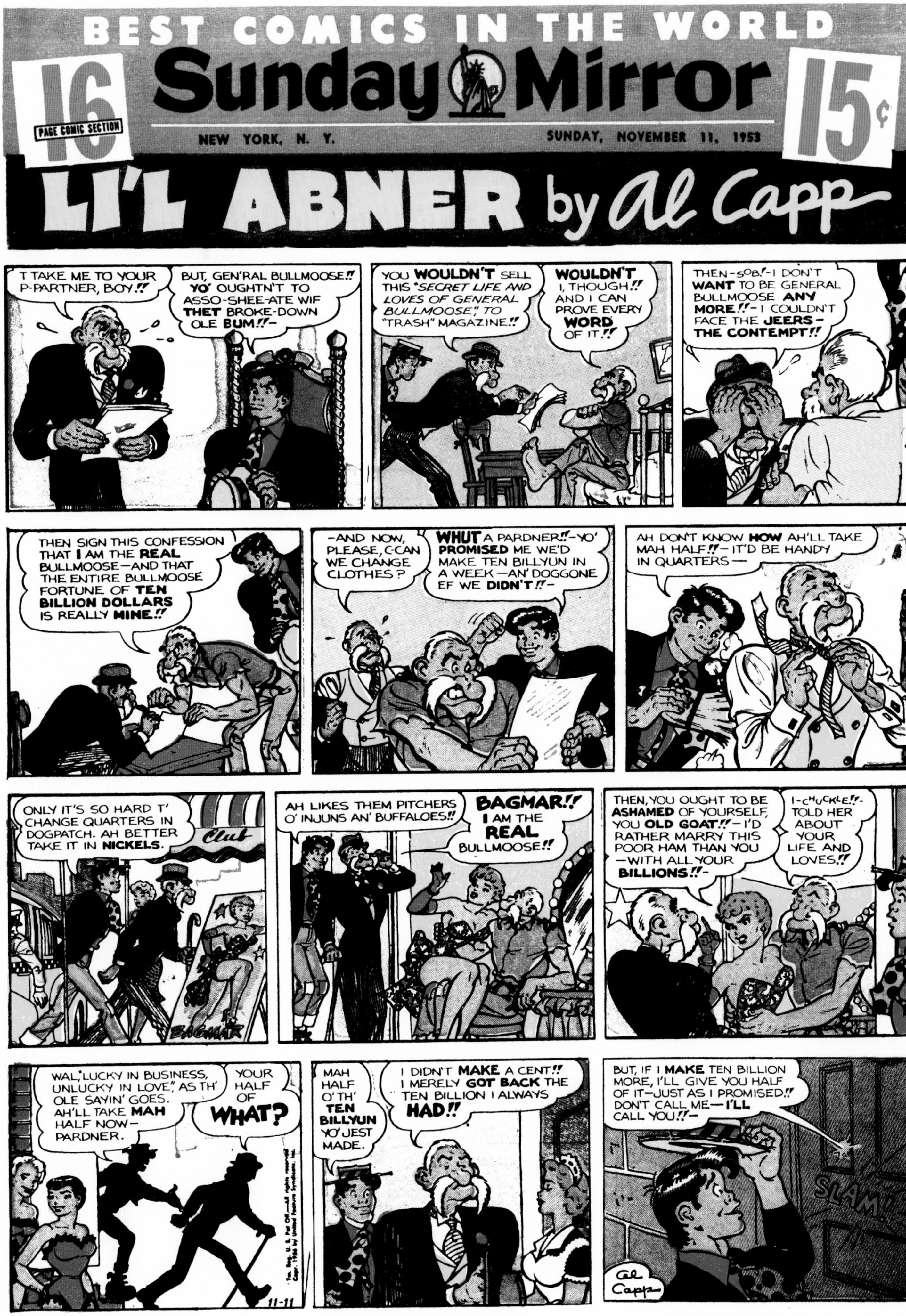
BEST COMICS IN THE WORLD
16 PAGE COMIC SECTION
Sunday Mirror
15¢
NEW YORK, N. Y.
SUNDAY, NOVEMBER 11, 1953
LI'L ABNER by Al Capp
T TAKE ME TO YOUR P-PARTNER, BOY!!
BUT, GEN'RAL BULLMOOSE!! YO' OUGHTN'T TO ASSO-SHEE-ATE WIF THET BROKE-DOWN OLE BUM!!-
YOU WOULDN'T SELL THIS "SECRET LIFE AND LOVES OF GENERAL BULLMOOSE," TO "TRASH" MAGAZINE!!
WOULDN'T I, THOUGH!! AND I CAN PROVE EVERY WORD OF IT!!
THEN-SOB!-I DON'T WANT TO BE GENERAL BULLMOOSE ANY MORE!!-I COULDN'T FACE THE JEERS-THE CONTEMPT!!
THEN SIGN THIS CONFESSION THAT I AM THE REAL BULLMOOSE-AND THAT THE ENTIRE BULLMOOSE FORTUNE OF TEN BILLION DOLLARS IS REALLY MINE!!
-AND NOW, PLEASE, C-CAN WE CHANGE CLOTHES?
WHUT A PARDNER!!-YO' PROMISED ME WE'D MAKE TEN BILLYUN IN A WEEK-AN' DOGGONE EF WE DIDN'T!!-
AH DON'T KNOW HOW AH'LL TAKE MAH HALF!!-IT'D BE HANDY IN QUARTERS-
ONLY IT'S SO HARD T' CHANGE QUARTERS IN DOGPATCH. AH BETTER TAKE IT IN NICKELS.
Club
BAGMAR
AH LIKES THEM PITCHERS O' INJUNS AN' BUFFALOES!!
BAGMAR!! I AM THE REAL BULLMOOSE!!
THEN, YOU OUGHT TO BE ASHAMED OF YOURSELF, YOU OLD GOAT!!-I'D RATHER MARRY THIS POOR HAM THAN YOU-WITH ALL YOUR BILLIONS!!-
I-CHUCKLE!!-TOLD HER ABOUT YOUR LIFE AND LOVES!!
WAL, "LUCKY IN BUSINESS, UNLUCKY IN LOVE," AS TH' OLE SAYIN' GOES. AH'LL TAKE MAH HALF NOW-PARDNER.
YOUR HALF OF WHAT?
11-11
MAH HALF O' TH' TEN BILLYUN YO' JEST MADE.
I DIDN'T MAKE A CENT!! I MERELY GOT BACK THE TEN BILLION I ALWAYS HAD!!
BUT, IF I MAKE TEN BILLION MORE, I'LL GIVE YOU HALF OF IT-JUST AS I PROMISED!! DON'T CALL ME-I'LL CALL YOU!!-
SLAM!
Al Capp

 **Sunday Mirror** 15¢

NEW YORK, N. Y.   SUNDAY, NOVEMBER 18, 1956

LI'L ABNER by Al Capp

19 COMICS

Sunday Mirror 15¢

NEW YORK, N. Y.   SUNDAY, NOVEMBER 25, 1956

LI'L ABNER by Al Capp

57

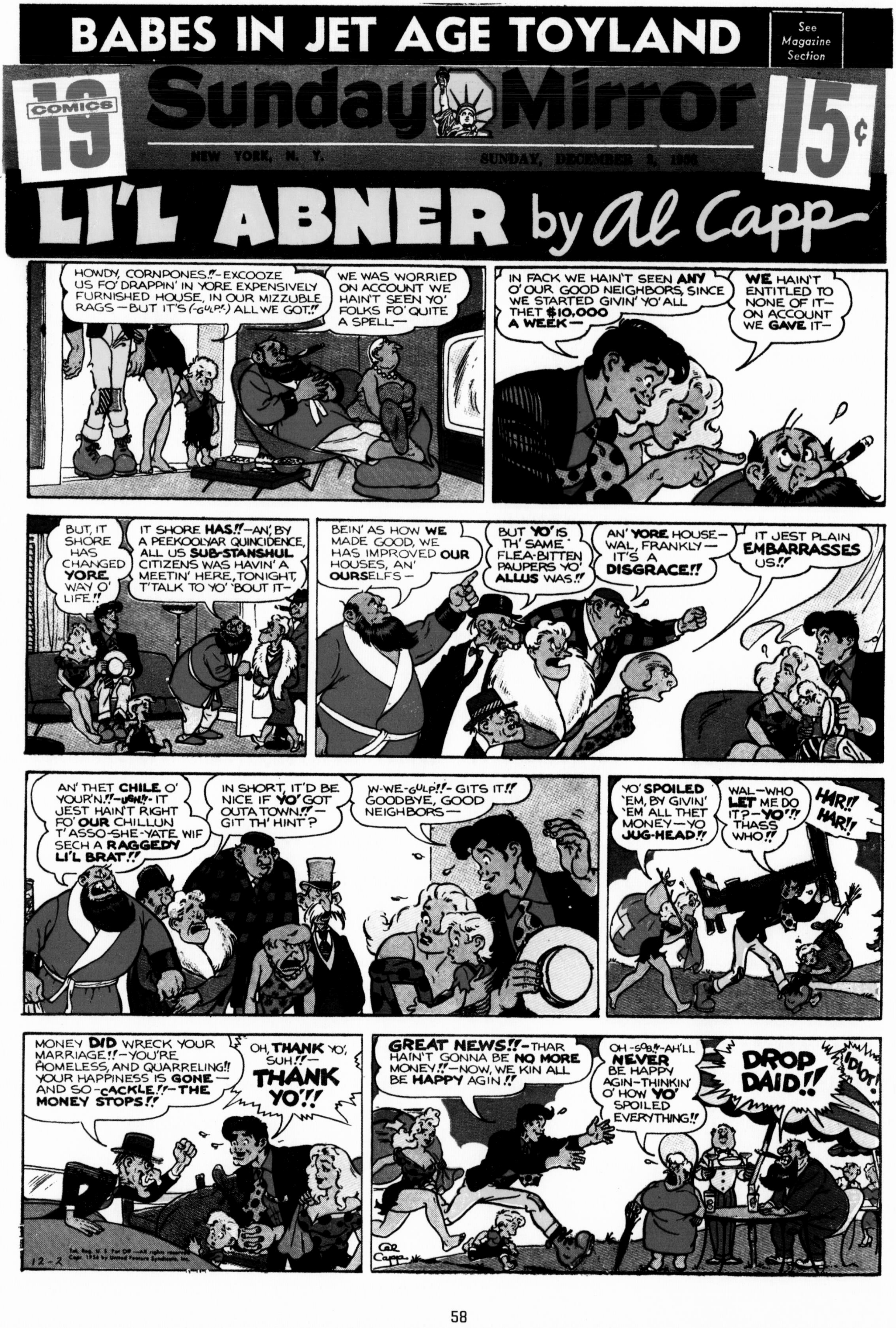

BABES IN JET AGE TOYLAND
See Magazine Section
19 COMICS
Sunday Mirror
15¢
NEW YORK, N. Y.
LI'L ABNER by Al Capp
HOWDY, CORNPONES!!-EXCOOZE US FO' DRAPPIN' IN YORE EXPENSIVELY FURNISHED HOUSE, IN OUR MIZZUBLE RAGS—BUT IT'S (-GULP!-) ALL WE GOT!!
WE WAS WORRIED ON ACCOUNT WE HAIN'T SEEN YO' FOLKS FO' QUITE A SPELL—
IN FACK WE HAIN'T SEEN ANY O' OUR GOOD NEIGHBORS, SINCE WE STARTED GIVIN' YO' ALL THET $10,000 A WEEK—
WE HAIN'T ENTITLED TO NONE OF IT—ON ACCOUNT WE GAVE IT—
BUT, IT SHORE HAS CHANGED YORE WAY O' LIFE!!
IT SHORE HAS!!-AN', BY A PEEKOOLYAR QUINCIDENCE, ALL US SUB-STANSHUL CITIZENS WAS HAVIN' A MEETIN' HERE, TONIGHT, T'TALK TO YO' 'BOUT IT—
BEIN' AS HOW WE MADE GOOD, WE HAS IMPROVED OUR HOUSES, AN' OURSELFS—
BUT YO' IS TH' SAME FLEA-BITTEN PAUPERS YO' ALLUS WAS!!
AN' YORE HOUSE-WAL, FRANKLY—IT'S A DISGRACE!!
IT JEST PLAIN EMBARRASSES US!!
AN' THET CHILE O' YOUR'N!!-UGH!!-IT JEST HAIN'T RIGHT FO' OUR CHILLUN T'ASSO-SHE-YATE WIF SECH A RAGGEDY LI'L BRAT!!
IN SHORT, IT'D BE NICE IF YO' GOT OUTA TOWN!!—GIT TH' HINT?
W-WE-GULP!!-GITS IT!! GOODBYE, GOOD NEIGHBORS—
YO' SPOILED 'EM, BY GIVIN' 'EM ALL THET MONEY—YO JUG-HEAD!!
WAL—WHO LET ME DO IT?—YO'!! THASS WHO!!
HAR!! HAR!!
MONEY DID WRECK YOUR MARRIAGE!!—YOU'RE HOMELESS, AND QUARRELING!! YOUR HAPPINESS IS GONE—AND SO-CACKLE!!—THE MONEY STOPS!!
OH, THANK YO', SUH!!—THANK YO'!!
12-2
GREAT NEWS!!—THAR HAIN'T GONNA BE NO MORE MONEY!!—NOW, WE KIN ALL BE HAPPY AGIN!!
OH-SOB!!-AH'LL NEVER BE HAPPY AGIN-THINKIN' O' HOW YO' SPOILED EVERYTHING!!
DROP DAID!!
IDIOT!
Al Capp

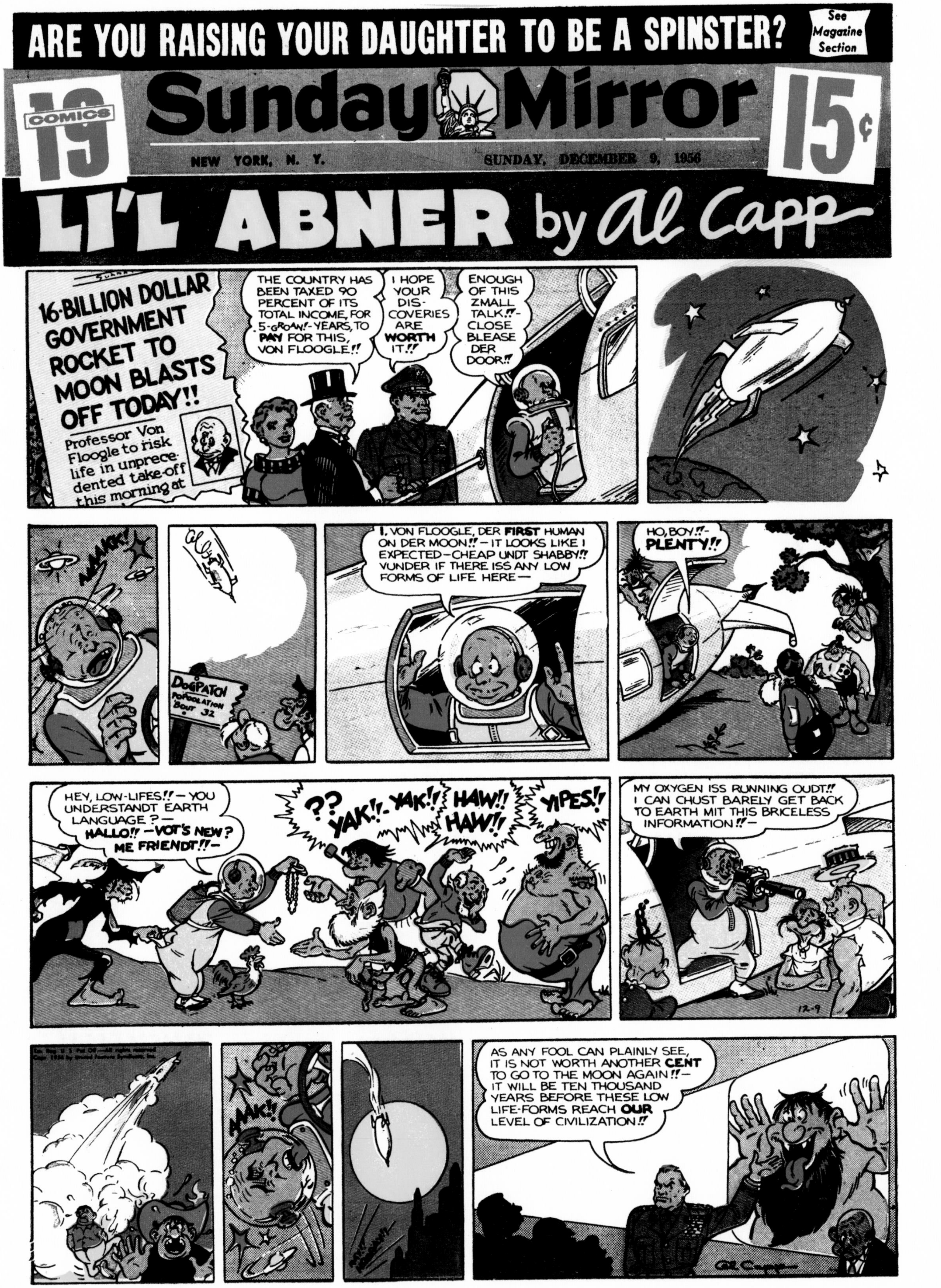
ARE YOU RAISING YOUR DAUGHTER TO BE A SPINSTER?
See Magazine Section
19 COMICS
Sunday Mirror
15¢
NEW YORK, N. Y.
SUNDAY, DECEMBER 9, 1956
LI'L ABNER by Al Capp
16-BILLION DOLLAR GOVERNMENT ROCKET TO MOON BLASTS OFF TODAY!!
Professor Von Floogle to risk life in unprecedented take-off this morning at
THE COUNTRY HAS BEEN TAXED 90 PERCENT OF ITS TOTAL INCOME, FOR 5-GROAN!-YEARS, TO PAY FOR THIS, VON FLOOGLE!!
I HOPE YOUR DISCOVERIES ARE WORTH IT!!
ENOUGH OF THIS ZMALL TALK!!-CLOSE BLEASE DER DOOR!!
AAAAK!
DOGPATCH POPOOLATION BOUT 32
I, VON FLOOGLE, DER FIRST HUMAN ON DER MOON!!-IT LOOKS LIKE I EXPECTED-CHEAP UNDT SHABBY!! VUNDER IF THERE ISS ANY LOW FORMS OF LIFE HERE—
HO, BOY!!-PLENTY!!
HEY, LOW-LIFES!!—YOU UNDERSTANDT EARTH LANGUAGE?—HALLO!!—VOT'S NEW? ME FRIENDT!!—
??
YAK!!-YAK!!
HAW!! HAW!!
YIPES!!
MY OXYGEN ISS RUNNING OUDT!! I CAN CHUST BARELY GET BACK TO EARTH MIT THIS BRICELESS INFORMATION!!—
12-9
AAAK!!
AS ANY FOOL CAN PLAINLY SEE, IT IS NOT WORTH ANOTHER CENT TO GO TO THE MOON AGAIN!!—IT WILL BE TEN THOUSAND YEARS BEFORE THESE LOW LIFE-FORMS REACH OUR LEVEL OF CIVILIZATION!!

Sunday Mirror

18 COMICS

15¢

NEW YORK, N. Y.   SUNDAY, DECEMBER 16, 1956

LI'L ABNER by Al Capp

 **Sunday Mirror** 15¢

NEW YORK, N.Y.   SUNDAY, DECEMBER 23, 1956

LI'L ABNER by Al Capp

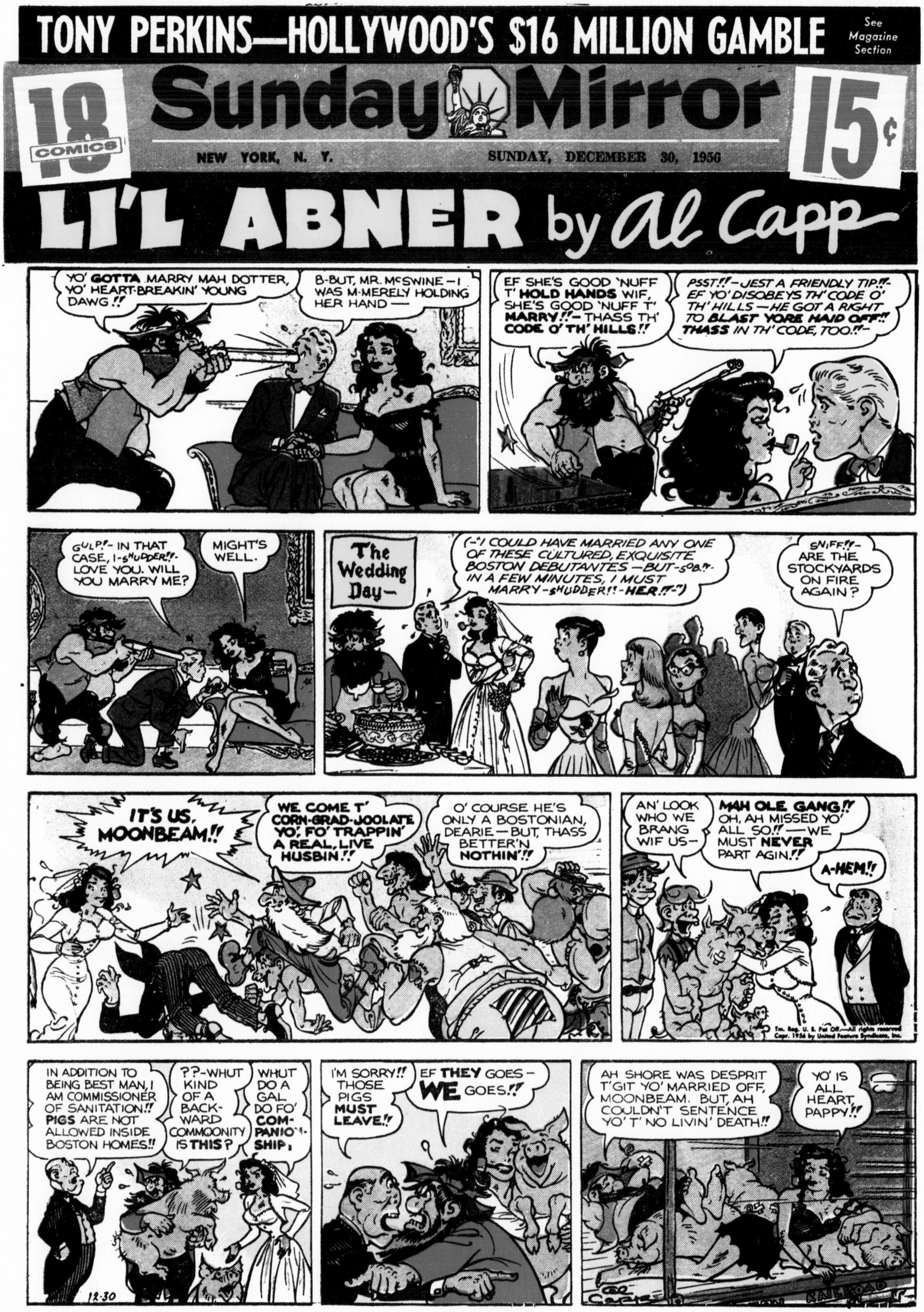
TONY PERKINS—HOLLYWOOD'S $16 MILLION GAMBLE
See Magazine Section
18 COMICS
Sunday Mirror
15¢
NEW YORK, N. Y.
SUNDAY, DECEMBER 30, 1956
LI'L ABNER by Al Capp
YO' GOTTA MARRY MAH DOTTER, YO' HEART-BREAKIN' YOUNG DAWG!!
B-BUT, MR. McSWINE—I WAS M-MERELY HOLDING HER HAND—
EF SHE'S GOOD 'NUFF T' HOLD HANDS WIF, SHE'S GOOD 'NUFF T' MARRY!!—THASS TH' CODE O' TH' HILLS!!
PSST!!—JEST A FRIENDLY TIP!!—EF YO' DISOBEYS TH' CODE O' TH' HILLS—HE GOT A RIGHT TO BLAST YORE HAID OFF!! THASS IN TH' CODE, TOO!!—
GULP!!—IN THAT CASE, I-SHUDDER!!—LOVE YOU. WILL YOU MARRY ME?
MIGHT'S WELL.
The Wedding Day—
(—"I COULD HAVE MARRIED ANY ONE OF THESE CULTURED, EXQUISITE BOSTON DEBUTANTES—BUT-SOB!!—IN A FEW MINUTES, I MUST MARRY-SHUDDER!!-HER!!—")
SNIFF!!—ARE THE STOCKYARDS ON FIRE AGAIN?
IT'S US, MOONBEAM!!
WE COME T' CORN-GRAD-JOOLATE YO', FO' TRAPPIN' A REAL, LIVE HUSBIN!!
O' COURSE HE'S ONLY A BOSTONIAN, DEARIE—BUT, THASS BETTER'N NOTHIN'!!
AN' LOOK WHO WE BRANG WIF US—
MAH OLE GANG!! OH, AH MISSED YO' ALL SO!!—WE MUST NEVER PART AGIN!!
A-HEM!!
Tm. Reg. U. S. Pat. Off.—All rights reserved Copr. 1956 by United Feature Syndicate, Inc.
IN ADDITION TO BEING BEST MAN, I AM COMMISSIONER OF SANITATION!! PIGS ARE NOT ALLOWED INSIDE BOSTON HOMES!!
??-WHUT KIND OF A BACK-WARD COMMOONITY IS THIS?
WHUT DO A GAL DO FO' COMPANIONSHIP,
12-30
I'M SORRY!! THOSE PIGS MUST LEAVE!!
EF THEY GOES—WE GOES!!
AH SHORE WAS DESPRIT T'GIT YO' MARRIED OFF, MOONBEAM. BUT, AH COULDN'T SENTENCE YO' T' NO LIVIN' DEATH!!
YO' IS ALL HEART, PAPPY!!
RAILROAD

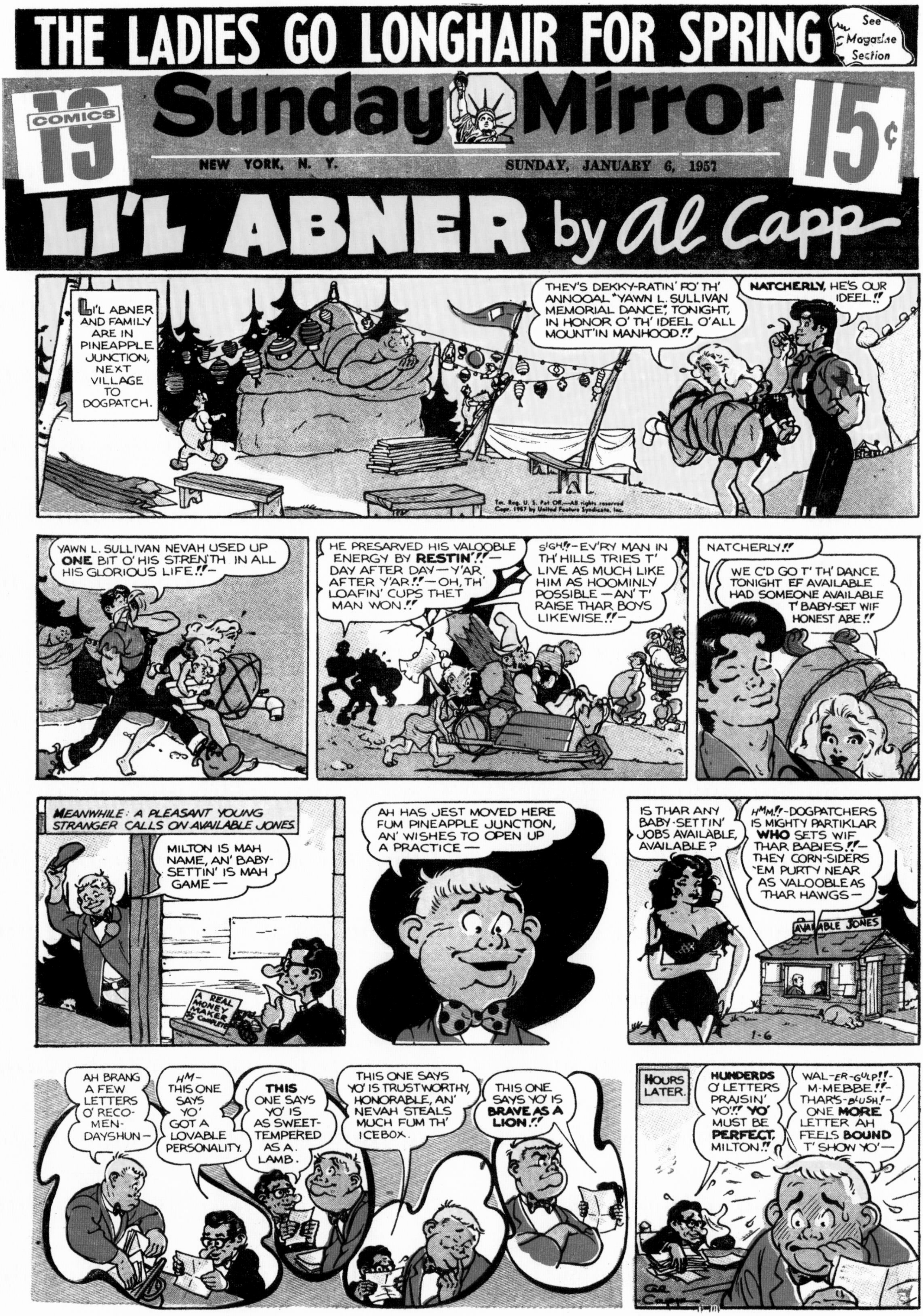
THE LADIES GO LONGHAIR FOR SPRING
See Magazine Section
19 COMICS
Sunday Mirror
15¢
NEW YORK, N. Y.
SUNDAY, JANUARY 6, 1957
LI'L ABNER by Al Capp
LI'L ABNER AND FAMILY ARE IN PINEAPPLE JUNCTION, NEXT VILLAGE TO DOGPATCH.
THEY'S DEKKY-RATIN' FO' TH' ANNOOAL "YAWN L. SULLIVAN MEMORIAL DANCE," TONIGHT, IN HONOR O' TH' IDEEL O'ALL MOUNT'IN MANHOOD!!
NATCHERLY, HE'S OUR IDEEL!!
YAWN L. SULLIVAN NEVAH USED UP ONE BIT O' HIS STRENTH IN ALL HIS GLORIOUS LIFE!!–
HE PRESARVED HIS VALOOBLE ENERGY BY RESTIN'!!– DAY AFTER DAY– Y'AR AFTER Y'AR!!– OH, TH' LOAFIN' CUPS THET MAN WON!!
SIGH!!– EV'RY MAN IN TH' HILLS TRIES T' LIVE AS MUCH LIKE HIM AS HOOMINLY POSSIBLE– AN' T' RAISE THAR BOYS LIKEWISE!!–
NATCHERLY!!
WE C'D GO T' TH' DANCE TONIGHT EF AVAILABLE HAD SOMEONE AVAILABLE T' BABY-SET WIF HONEST ABE!!
MEANWHILE: A PLEASANT YOUNG STRANGER CALLS ON AVAILABLE JONES.
MILTON IS MAH NAME, AN' BABY-SETTIN' IS MAH GAME–
A REAL MONEY MAKER
AH HAS JEST MOVED HERE FUM PINEAPPLE JUNCTION, AN' WISHES TO OPEN UP A PRACTICE–
IS THAR ANY BABY-SETTIN' JOBS AVAILABLE, AVAILABLE?
HMM!!– DOGPATCHERS IS MIGHTY PARTIKLAR WHO SETS WIF THAR BABIES!!– THEY CORN-SIDERS 'EM PURTY NEAR AS VALOOBLE AS THAR HAWGS–
AVAILABLE JONES
AH BRANG A FEW LETTERS O' RECOMMEN-DAYSHUN–
HM– THIS ONE SAYS YO' GOT A LOVABLE PERSONALITY.
THIS ONE SAYS YO' IS AS SWEET-TEMPERED AS A LAMB.
THIS ONE SAYS YO' IS TRUSTWORTHY, HONORABLE, AN' NEVAH STEALS MUCH FUM TH' ICEBOX.
THIS ONE SAYS YO' IS BRAVE AS A LION!!
HOURS LATER.
HUNDERDS O' LETTERS PRAISIN' YO'!! YO' MUST BE PERFECT, MILTON!!
WAL-ER-GULP!!– M-MEBBE!!– THAR'S-BLUSH!– ONE MORE LETTER AH FEELS BOUND T' SHOW YO'–

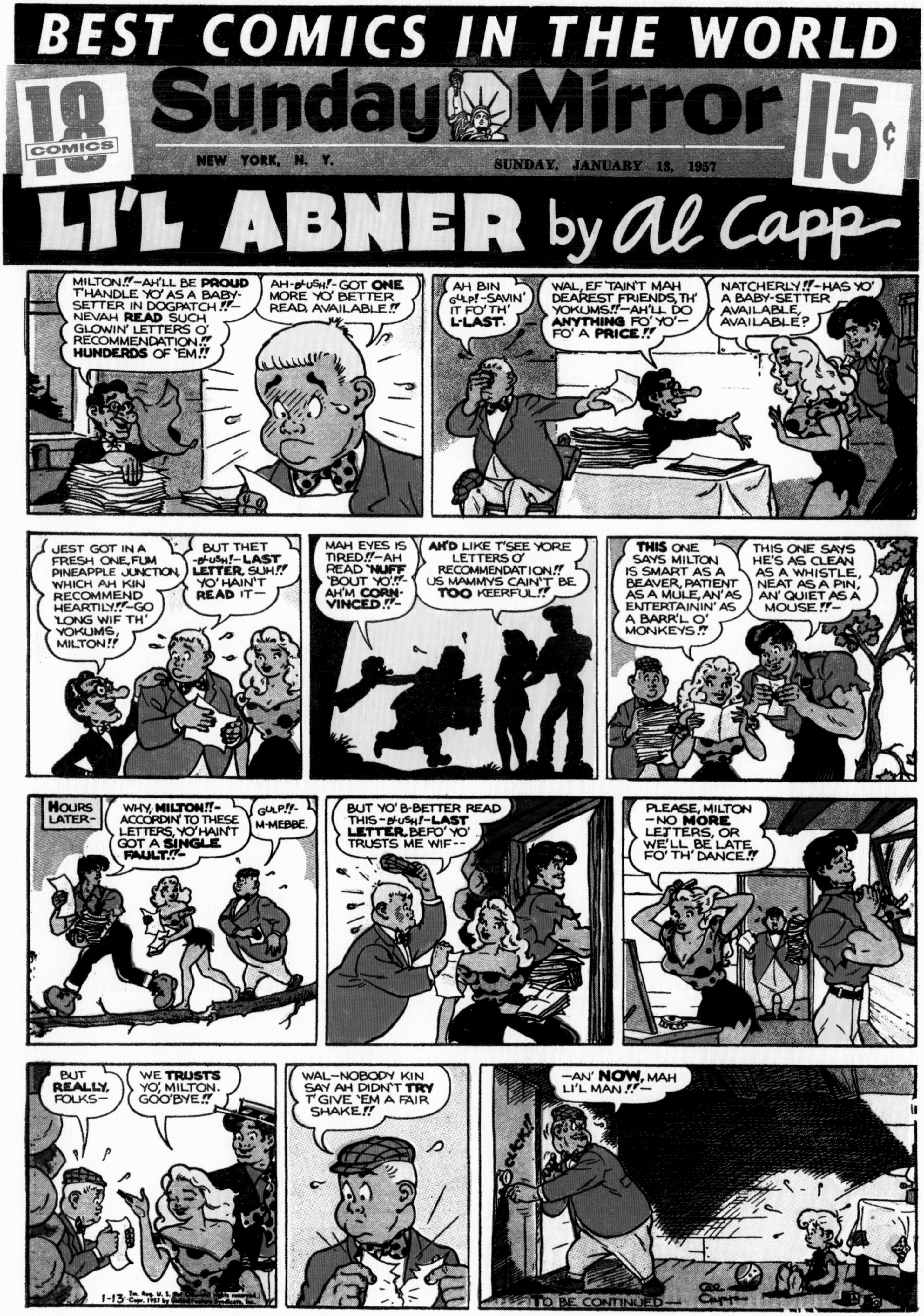

BEST COMICS IN THE WORLD
18 COMICS
Sunday Mirror
15¢
NEW YORK, N. Y.
SUNDAY, JANUARY 13, 1957
LI'L ABNER by Al Capp
MILTON!!–AH'LL BE PROUD T'HANDLE YO' AS A BABY-SETTER IN DOGPATCH!!–NEVAH READ SUCH GLOWIN' LETTERS O' RECOMMENDATION!! HUNDERDS OF 'EM!!
AH-BLUSH!-GOT ONE MORE YO' BETTER READ, AVAILABLE.!!
AH BIN GULP!-SAVIN' IT FO' TH' L-LAST.
WAL, EF 'TAIN'T MAH DEAREST FRIENDS, TH' YOKUMS!!–AH'LL DO ANYTHING FO' YO'– FO' A PRICE!!
NATCHERLY!!–HAS YO' A BABY-SETTER AVAILABLE, AVAILABLE?
JEST GOT IN A FRESH ONE, FUM PINEAPPLE JUNCTION, WHICH AH KIN RECOMMEND HEARTILY!!–GO 'LONG WIF TH' YOKUMS, MILTON!!
BUT THET -BLUSH!- LAST LETTER, SUH!! YO' HAIN'T READ IT—
MAH EYES IS TIRED!!–AH READ 'NUFF 'BOUT YO'!!– AH'M CORNVINCED!!–
AH'D LIKE T'SEE YORE LETTERS O' RECOMMENDATION!! US MAMMYS CAIN'T BE TOO KEERFUL!!
THIS ONE SAYS MILTON IS SMART AS A BEAVER, PATIENT AS A MULE, AN' AS ENTERTAININ' AS A BARR'L O' MONKEYS!!
THIS ONE SAYS HE'S AS CLEAN AS A WHISTLE, NEAT AS A PIN, AN' QUIET AS A MOUSE!!–
HOURS LATER–
WHY, MILTON!!– ACCORDIN' TO THESE LETTERS, YO' HAIN'T GOT A SINGLE FAULT!!–
GULP!!– M-MEBBE.
BUT YO' B-BETTER READ THIS-BLUSH!-LAST LETTER, BEFO' YO' TRUSTS ME WIF--
PLEASE, MILTON —NO MORE LETTERS, OR WE'LL BE LATE FO' TH' DANCE!!
BUT REALLY, FOLKS—
WE TRUSTS YO', MILTON. GOO'BYE!!
WAL–NOBODY KIN SAY AH DIDN'T TRY T'GIVE 'EM A FAIR SHAKE!!
—AN' NOW, MAH LI'L MAN!!—
CLICK!!
TO BE CONTINUED—

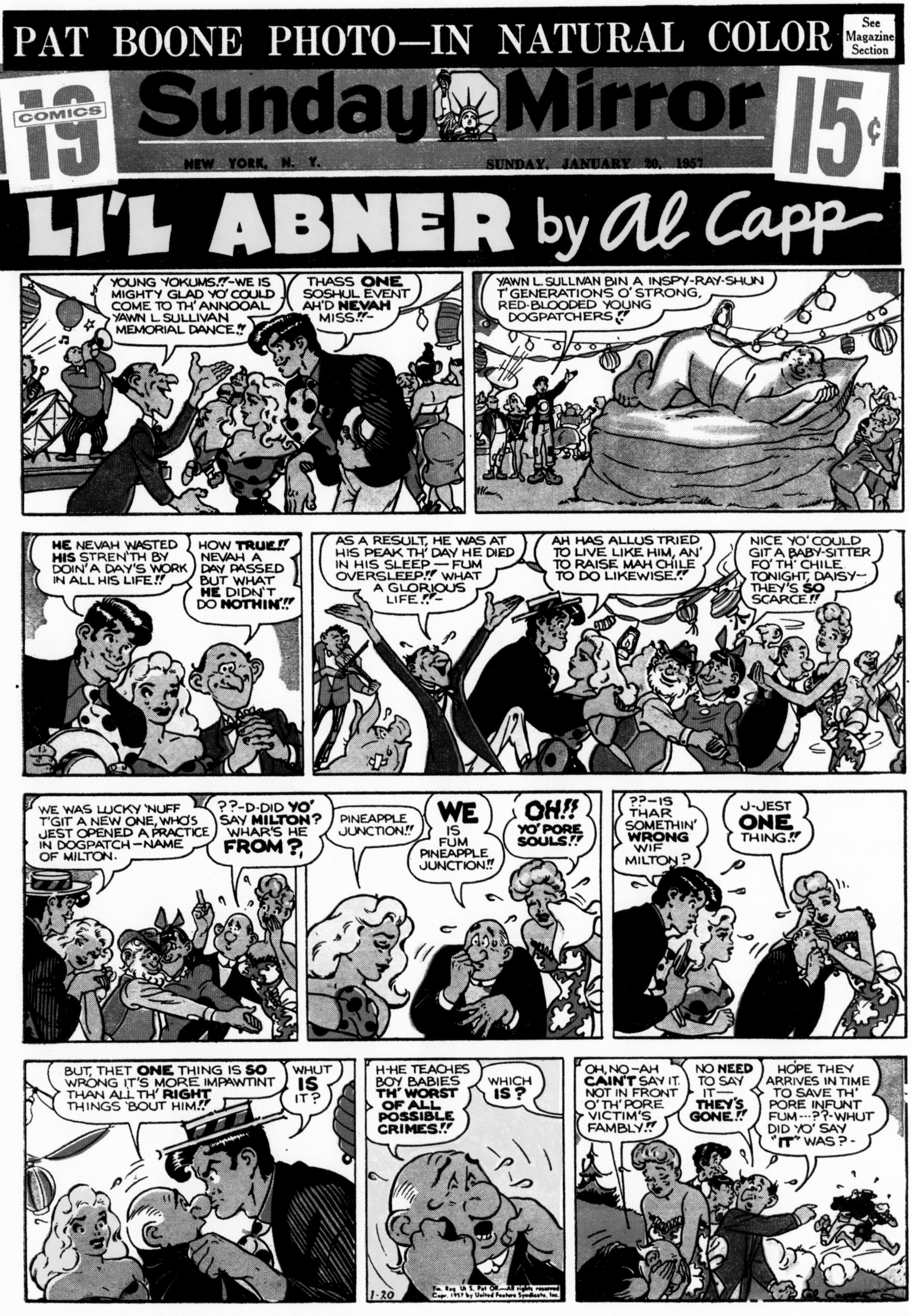
PAT BOONE PHOTO—IN NATURAL COLOR
See Magazine Section
COMICS
19
Sunday Mirror
NEW YORK, N. Y.
SUNDAY, JANUARY 20, 1957
15¢
LI'L ABNER by Al Capp
YOUNG YOKUMS!!-WE IS MIGHTY GLAD YO' COULD COME TO TH' ANNOOAL YAWN L. SULLIVAN MEMORIAL DANCE!!
THASS ONE SOSHUL EVENT AH'D NEVAH MISS!!-
YAWN L. SULLIVAN BIN A INSPY-RAY-SHUN T'GENERATIONS O' STRONG, RED-BLOODED YOUNG DOGPATCHERS!!
HE NEVAH WASTED HIS STREN'TH BY DOIN' A DAY'S WORK IN ALL HIS LIFE!!
HOW TRUE!! NEVAH A DAY PASSED BUT WHAT HE DIDN'T DO NOTHIN'!!
AS A RESULT, HE WAS AT HIS PEAK TH' DAY HE DIED IN HIS SLEEP — FUM OVERSLEEP!! WHAT A GLORIOUS LIFE!!-
AH HAS ALLUS TRIED TO LIVE LIKE HIM, AN' TO RAISE MAH CHILE TO DO LIKEWISE!!
NICE YO' COULD GIT A BABY-SITTER FO' TH' CHILE TONIGHT, DAISY— THEY'S SO SCARCE!!
WE WAS LUCKY 'NUFF T'GIT A NEW ONE, WHO'S JEST OPENED A PRACTICE IN DOGPATCH—NAME OF MILTON.
??-D-DID YO' SAY MILTON? WHAR'S HE FROM?
PINEAPPLE JUNCTION!!
WE IS FUM PINEAPPLE JUNCTION!!
OH!! YO' PORE SOULS!!
??-IS THAR SOMETHIN' WRONG WIF MILTON?
J-JEST ONE THING!!
BUT, THET ONE THING IS SO WRONG IT'S MORE IMPAWTINT THAN ALL TH' RIGHT THINGS 'BOUT HIM!!
WHUT IS IT?
H-HE TEACHES BOY BABIES TH' WORST OF ALL POSSIBLE CRIMES!!
WHICH IS?
OH, NO-AH CAIN'T SAY IT. NOT IN FRONT O' TH' PORE VICTIM'S FAMBLY!!
NO NEED TO SAY IT— THEY'S GONE!!
HOPE THEY ARRIVES IN TIME TO SAVE TH' PORE INFUNT FUM---??-WHUT DID YO' SAY "IT" WAS?-
1-20
Tm. Reg. U.S. Pat. Off.—All rights reserved
Copr. 1957 by United Feature Syndicate, Inc.

THE FASHION PIRATES WHO RAID 5TH AVE. See Magazine Section

18 COMICS

Sunday Mirror

NEW YORK, N. Y.   SUNDAY, JANUARY 27, 1957

15¢

LI'L ABNER by Al Capp

LI'L ABNER
by
AL CAPP ®

RARE BIRDS MAGAZINE

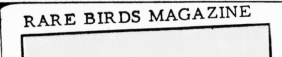

THE BASHFUL BULGANIK

Can be seen only in Slobbovia, where it can't be seen either. It flies too fast, and is terribly bashful.

This is one of the clearest photos ever made of a Bashful Bulganik in flight.

IT'S BEAUTIFUL!!—JUST BEAUTIFUL—??—ER—WHO ARE YOU, BOY?

NAME OF LI'L ABNER YOKUM, GENERAL BULLMOOSE, SUH!! YORE NEW BODYGUARD!!

WISH'T AH WAS RICH, AN' HAD A YACHT LIKE YO'—AN' COULD GO T' SLOBBOVIA, AN' SEE A REAL, LIVE BASHFUL BULGANIK!!

'STEAD O' JEST SETTIN' HERE, AN' MERELY LOOKIN' AT A PITCHER O' ONE, LIKE A IDIOT!!

THAT'S A SPLENDID IDEA, BOY!! LET'S GO!!

A MONTH LATER — SLOBBOVIA.

WHERE ARE ALL THE BASHFUL BULGANIKS?

WHERE AIN'T THEY? YOU'RE STANDING IN THE MIDDLE OF A BUNCH OF THEM!!

HE'S RIGHT!!—THAR MUST BE MILLYUNS OF 'EM AROUN', ON ACCOUNT YO' CAIN'T SEE NOTHIN'!!

MY!! THEY'S FAST!!

SIGH!!—EF AH WERE A RICH OLE COOT LIKE YO', SUH, AH'D BUY MAHSELF A BASHFUL BULGANIK, 'STEAD O' STANDIN' 'ROUND HERE AN' GAWKIN' AT 'EM, LIKE A IDIOT!!

I'M GLAD YOU SUGGESTED THAT, BOY!!

WHERE CAN I PURCHASE A BASHFUL BULGANIK, SHORTY?

YOU GOT TO MAKE A DILL WITH THE COMMISSIONER OF WILD LIFE, WHO WOULD BE WERRY DIFFICULT TO CONTACT—EXCEPT I HIM!!

A BASHFUL BULGANIK WILL COSTING YOU 1,000 RASBUCKNIKS, NATIONAL CURRENCY OF SLOBBOVIA.

A RASBUCKNIK HAIN'T WORTH NOTHIN'—SO, IN AMERICAN MONEY THET COMES TO—??—SHECKS!—GIVE HIM A DOLLAH!!

2-3

IS THERE ONE INSIDE?

NOTCHERLY!! YOU CAN'T SEE NOTHING, SO THERE MUST BE ONE THERE!!

BACK ON THE YACHT—

CHUCKLE!!—SNORT!! I'VE NEVER HAD SO MUCH FUN IN MY LIFE! ITS SPEED IS FANTASTIC!!

AND IT'S SO QUIET!! YO'D NEVAH KNOW IT WAS THAR!!

BULGANIK

TO BE CONTINUED

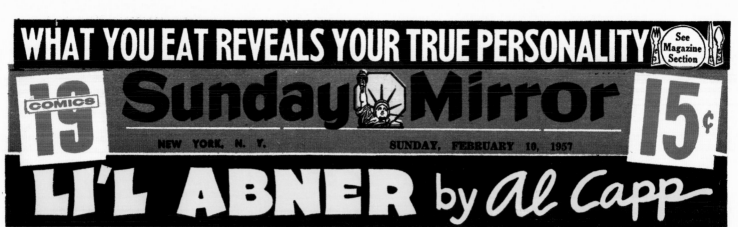

COMICS 19 Sunday Mirror 15¢

NEW YORK, N. Y.   SUNDAY, FEBRUARY 10, 1957

LI'L ABNER by Al Capp

19 COMICS — Sunday Mirror — 15¢

NEW YORK, N. Y.   SUNDAY, FEBRUARY 17, 1957

LI'L ABNER by Al Capp

LI'L ABNER
by
AL CAPP ®

YOUSE ARE DE 'BOSS OF DIS MOB, BIG STANISLOUSE!!

AN' US CRUMBS GOES ALONG WIT' WHATSOEVER YOU FANCIES—

BUT, FRANKLY, WE ARE TIRED O' SUPPORTIN' YOUR BRUDDER, "FOUR-EYES"!!

HE DON'T DO NUTTIN' BUT READ!!

YOU LEAVE FOUR-EYES ALONE.!! FROM READING SOMET'ING GOOD IS GONNA COME.!! WAIT AN' SEE.!!—

FIVE YEARS LATER— WE HATES TO NAG YOU, BIG STANISLOUSE, BUT DAT BUM OF A BRUDDER O' YOURS IS STILL READIN'!!

—AN' WHAT GOOD HAS COME OF IT?—

HM!!—HERE'S AN INTERESTING HISTORICAL FACT—

GENERAL JUBILATION T. CORNPONE, DOGPATCH'S GREATEST MILITARY FIGURE, HERO OF SUCH IMMORTAL BATTLES AS---

"CORNPONE'S DISASTER," "CORNPONE'S RETREAT," "CORNPONE'S ROUT," "CORNPONE'S HUMILIATION," AND "CORNPONE'S LAST STAND."—

WAS PRESENTED WITH A DIAMOND-STUDDED BELT BY THE RAJAH OF HYDUNDERABAD, IN 1870—

AFTER CORNPONE WAS KICKED TO DEATH IN 1880 BY AN UNFRIENDLY COW, A STATUE WAS ERECTED TO HIM. IN DOGPATCH—AND THE DIAMOND-STUDDED BELT WAS PLACED ON IT!!

THE BELT IS STILL THERE— AND IS NOW WORTH OVER A MILLION DOLLARS!!

SEE!!—YOU CRUMBS!! FROM READIN' HE GOT THAT TIP!!

MEANWHILE—IN DOGPATCH—

ANY BIRD WHAT DAST FLY OVER THET HONORED STATCHOO GITS IT BETWIXT TH' EYES!!

A RAINDROP!! IT MUSTN'T FALL ON HIM.

GOTTA PROTECK HIM FUM TH' SUN.

US DOG-PATCHERS WOULD GLADLY DIE T' DEFEND THET STATCHOO!!

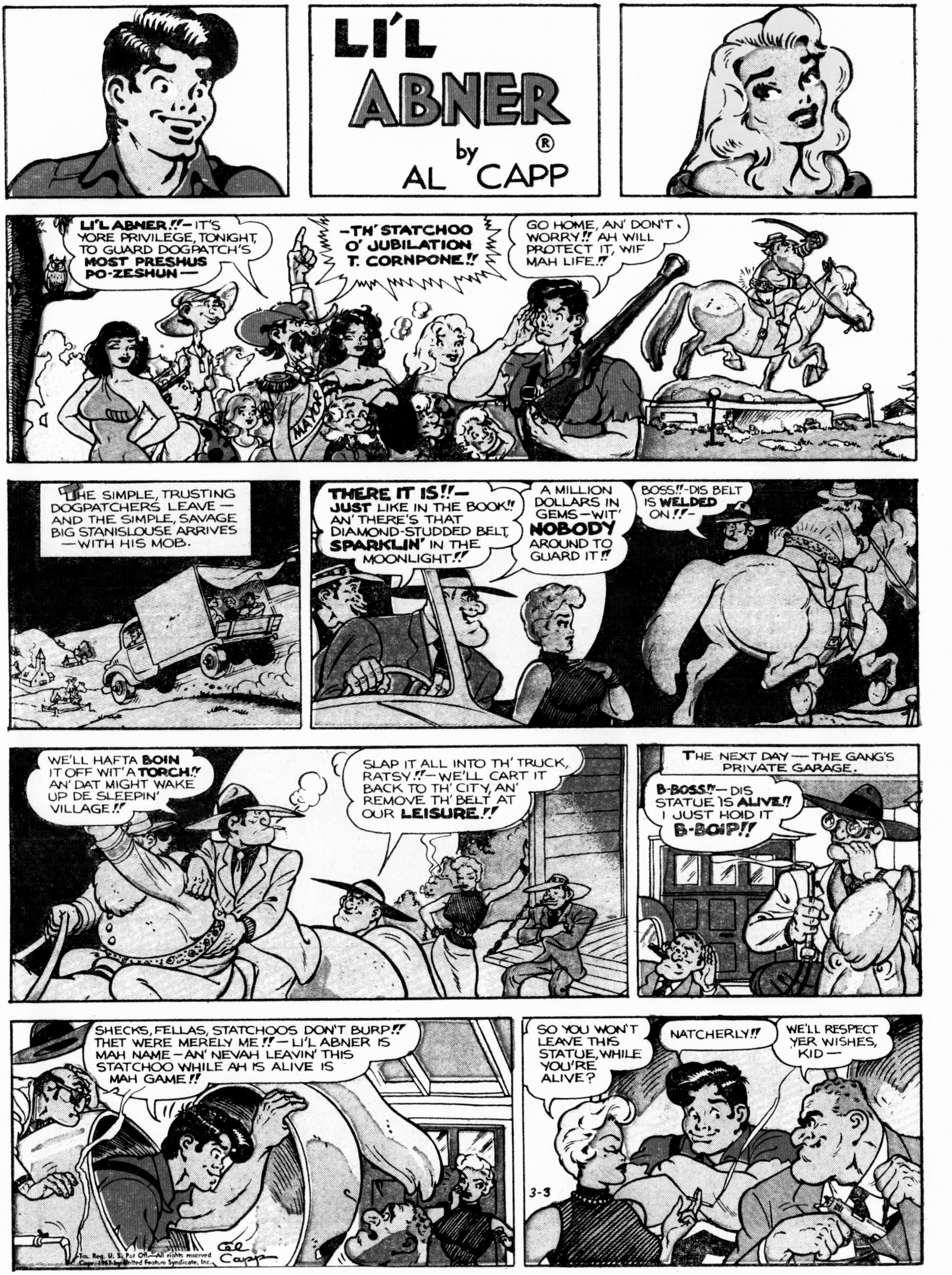
LI'L ABNER
by AL CAPP ®
LI'L ABNER!!—IT'S YORE PRIVILEGE, TONIGHT, TO GUARD DOGPATCH'S MOST PRESHUS PO-ZESHUN—
—TH' STATCHOO O' JUBILATION T. CORNPONE!!
GO HOME, AN' DON'T WORRY!! AH WILL PROTECT IT, WIF MAH LIFE!!
MAYOR
THE SIMPLE, TRUSTING DOGPATCHERS LEAVE—AND THE SIMPLE, SAVAGE BIG STANISLOUSE ARRIVES—WITH HIS MOB.
THERE IT IS!!—JUST LIKE IN THE BOOK!! AN' THERE'S THAT DIAMOND-STUDDED BELT, SPARKLIN' IN THE MOONLIGHT!!
A MILLION DOLLARS IN GEMS—WIT' NOBODY AROUND TO GUARD IT!!
BOSS!!-DIS BELT IS WELDED ON!!-
WE'LL HAFTA BOIN IT OFF WIT' A TORCH!! AN' DAT MIGHT WAKE UP DE SLEEPIN' VILLAGE!!
SLAP IT ALL INTO TH' TRUCK, RATSY!!—WE'LL CART IT BACK TO TH' CITY, AN' REMOVE TH' BELT AT OUR LEISURE!!
THE NEXT DAY—THE GANG'S PRIVATE GARAGE.
B-BOSS!!—DIS STATUE IS ALIVE!! I JUST HOID IT B-BOIP!!
SHECKS, FELLAS, STATCHOOS DON'T BURP!! THET WERE MERELY ME!!—LI'L ABNER IS MAH NAME—AN' NEVAH LEAVIN' THIS STATCHOO WHILE AH IS ALIVE IS MAH GAME!!
Tm. Reg. U. S. Pat Off.—All rights reserved
Copr. 1957 by United Feature Syndicate, Inc.
Al Capp
3-3
SO YOU WON'T LEAVE THIS STATUE, WHILE YOU'RE ALIVE?
NATCHERLY!!
WE'LL RESPECT YER WISHES, KID—

Sunday Mirror

18 COMICS — 15¢

NEW YORK, N. Y. — SUNDAY, MARCH 10, 1957

LI'L ABNER by Al Capp

Li'L ABNER. Up in Ruthie's room— by AL CAPP

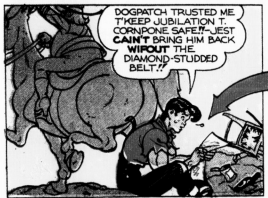

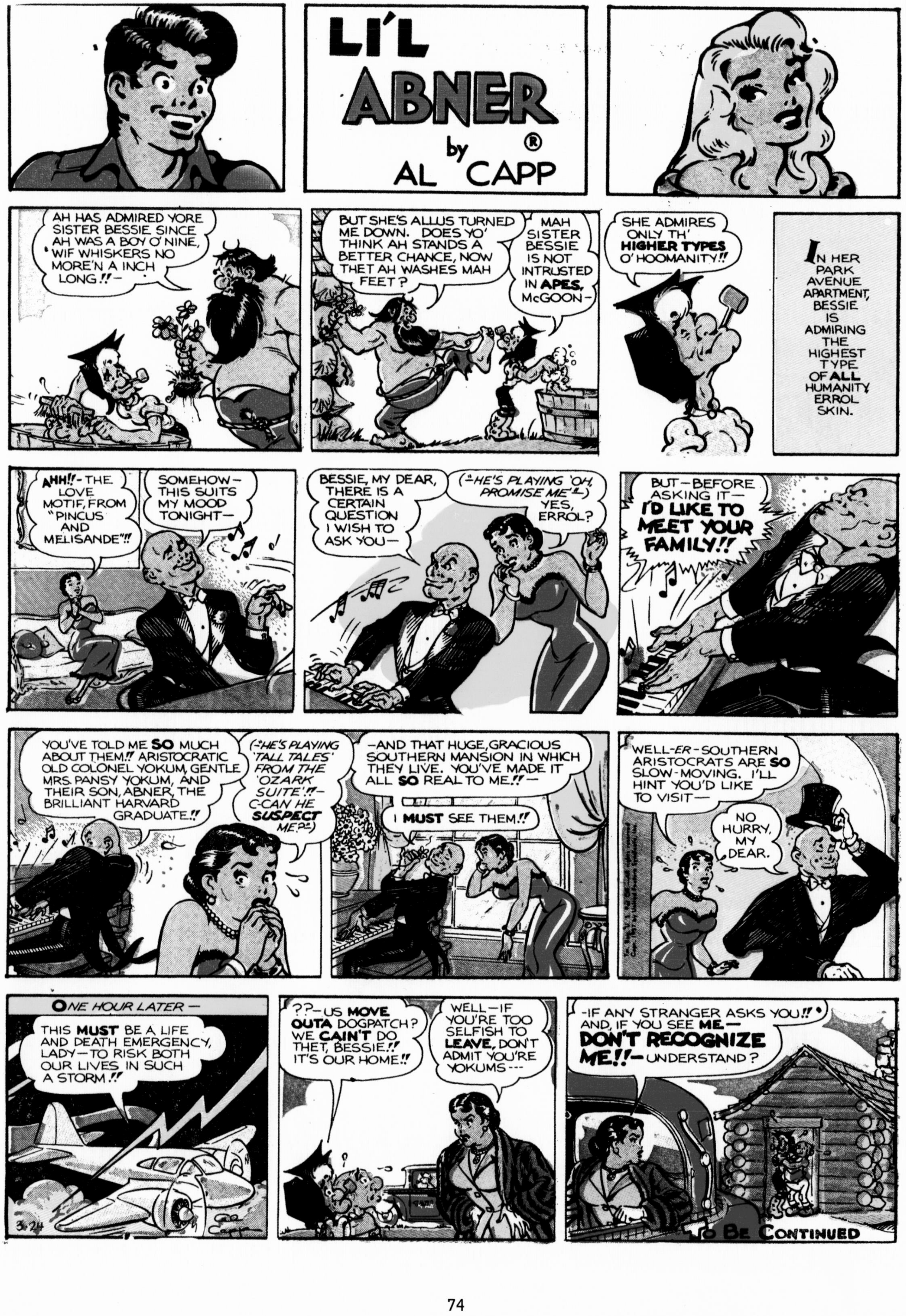
LI'L ABNER
by AL CAPP ®
AH HAS ADMIRED YORE SISTER BESSIE SINCE AH WAS A BOY O' NINE, WIF WHISKERS NO MORE'N A INCH LONG!!—
BUT SHE'S ALLUS TURNED ME DOWN. DOES YO' THINK AH STANDS A BETTER CHANCE, NOW THET AH WASHES MAH FEET?
MAH SISTER BESSIE IS NOT INTRUSTED IN APES, McGOON—
SHE ADMIRES ONLY TH' HIGHER TYPES O' HOOMANITY!!
IN HER PARK AVENUE APARTMENT, BESSIE IS ADMIRING THE HIGHEST TYPE OF ALL HUMANITY, ERROL SKIN.
AHH!!—THE LOVE MOTIF, FROM "PINCUS AND MELISANDE"!!
SOMEHOW—THIS SUITS MY MOOD TONIGHT—
BESSIE, MY DEAR, THERE IS A CERTAIN QUESTION I WISH TO ASK YOU—
(—HE'S PLAYING 'OH, PROMISE ME'—) YES, ERROL?
BUT—BEFORE ASKING IT— I'D LIKE TO MEET YOUR FAMILY!!
YOU'VE TOLD ME SO MUCH ABOUT THEM!! ARISTOCRATIC OLD COLONEL YOKUM, GENTLE MRS. PANSY YOKUM, AND THEIR SON, ABNER, THE BRILLIANT HARVARD GRADUATE!!
(—HE'S PLAYING 'TALL TALES' FROM THE 'OZARK SUITE'!!— C-CAN HE SUSPECT ME?—)
—AND THAT HUGE, GRACIOUS SOUTHERN MANSION IN WHICH THEY LIVE. YOU'VE MADE IT ALL SO REAL TO ME!!—
I MUST SEE THEM!!
WELL—ER—SOUTHERN ARISTOCRATS ARE SO SLOW-MOVING. I'LL HINT YOU'D LIKE TO VISIT—
NO HURRY, MY DEAR.
ONE HOUR LATER—
THIS MUST BE A LIFE AND DEATH EMERGENCY, LADY—TO RISK BOTH OUR LIVES IN SUCH A STORM!!
??—US MOVE OUTA DOGPATCH? WE CAIN'T DO THET, BESSIE!! IT'S OUR HOME!!
WELL—IF YOU'RE TOO SELFISH TO LEAVE, DON'T ADMIT YOU'RE YOKUMS---
-IF ANY STRANGER ASKS YOU!! AND, IF YOU SEE ME— DON'T RECOGNIZE ME!!—UNDERSTAND?
TO BE CONTINUED

LI'L ABNER
by AL CAPP ®

WE'LL DO LIKE YO' SAY!! WE WON'T ADMIT TO **ANY** STRANGER WE IS YOKUMS!!

GOOD!!

AN' EF WE SEES YO'—AN' YO' DON'T SPEAK TO US —**WE'LL** UNDERSTAND.

WE KNOWS YO' LOVES US, BESSIE— AN' ALL THIS IS PROB'LY FO' OUR OWN GOOD.

BACK IN N.Y.—A CONSTRUCTION Co.—

MONEY IS NO OBJECT!!—BUY THE SOUTH'S FINEST MANSION, AND MOVE IT TO DOGPATCH.!!—

A THEATRICAL AGENCY.

YOU WISH TO CAST A **COMPLETE FAMILY**?—ANY **SPECIAL** STARS?

A SIR LAURENCE OLIVIER TYPE WILL DO FOR PAPPY YOKUM— AND---

—KATHERINE CORNELL FOR MAMMY. ROCK HUDSON, OF COURSE, MUST PLAY LI'L ABNER —AND EDIE ADAMS, FOR DAISY MAE!!

THAT'LL BE A PRETTY EXPENSIVE CAST, MADAME—

—BUT, WITH ·GASP!!·—**THIS** CHECK—**THEY'LL ALL BE THERE**—MINT JULEPS IN HAND, AND "YOU-ALL"ING FIT TO BUST!!

WITHIN A FEW DAYS, ERROL SKIN RECEIVES

Colonel and Mrs. Lucifer Ornamental Yokum request your presence for the week end, at their palatial southern mansion, "Magnolia Hall," Dogpatch.
R.S.V.P.

SO **THAT'S** YOUR ANCESTRAL HOME.!!— MAGNIFICENT!!

(—"IT **OUGHT** TO BE. IT'S COSTING ME $100,000 FOR THE WEEK-END.!!"—)

??!—WHAT A **PRICELESS** LITTLE CABIN! LET'S STOP—

REALLY, MY DEAR—IT'S **SQUALID.!!**— AND THOSE PEOPLE.!!— THEY'RE **HARDLY HUMAN** !!

ON THE CONTRARY.!! THEY'RE **CHARMING.!!** I'VE NEVER SEEN ANYTHING SO QUAINT IN ALL MY LIFE.!!—

AN' **WE** NEVAH SEEN **HER** IN ALL OUR LIFES— HONEST!!

HAS WE, PAPPY?

SHECKS, NO.!! WE NEVAH EVAH LAID EYES ON TH'OLE BAT.!!—

PLEASE.!!—WE **MUST** GET ON TO THE PALATIAL MANSION OF MY ARISTOCRATIC RELATIVES.!!"

THASS RIGHT, BESSIE—ᴱᴿ—AH MEANS "STRANGER".!!—IF YO' WANTS T'MAKE A GOOD IMPRESHUN ON THET BOY— BRING HIM UP TO THET BRAND-NEW OLD SOUTHERN MANSHUN ON TH' HILL—

3-31

TO BE CONTINUED:

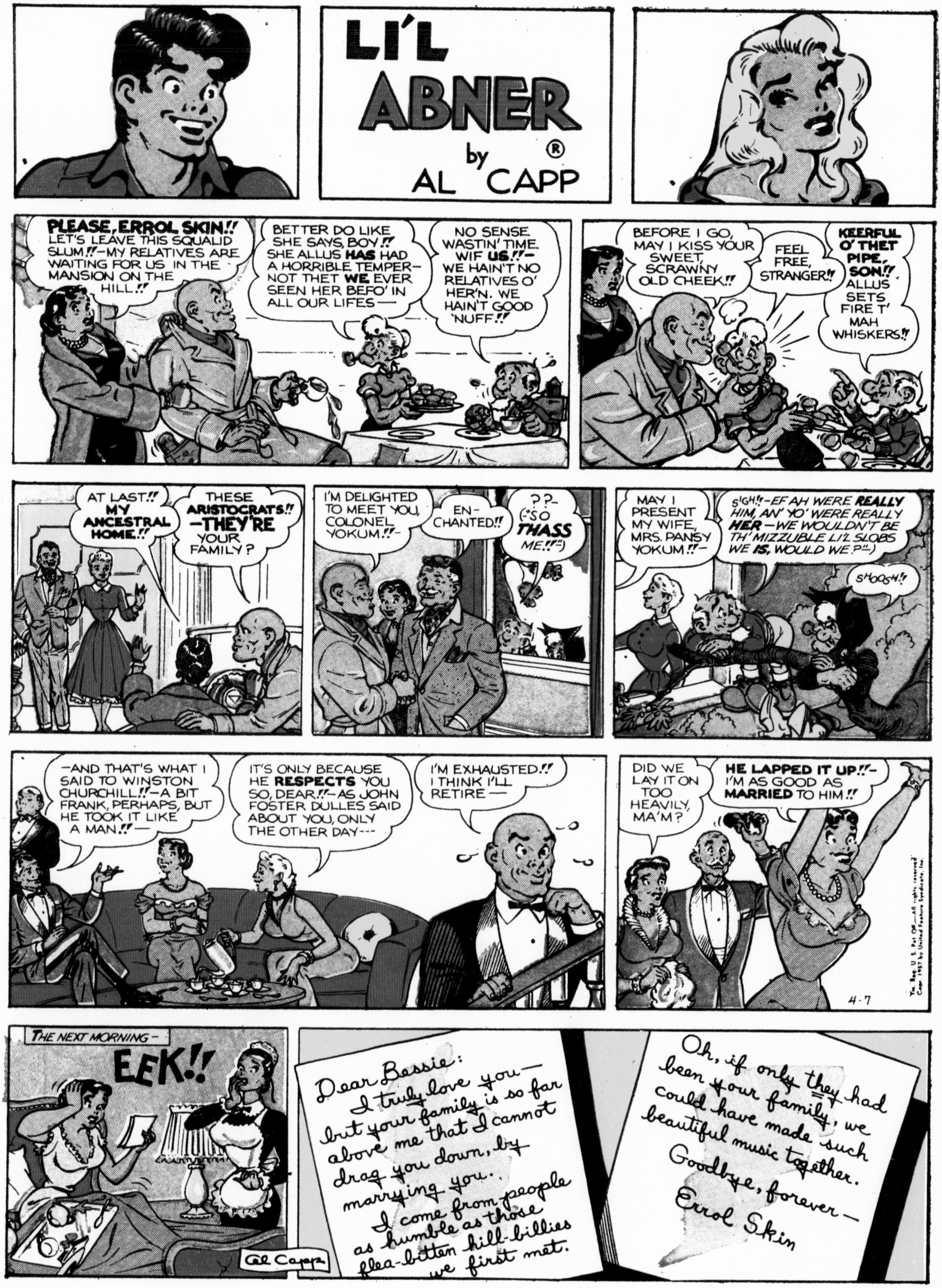
LI'L ABNER
by AL CAPP ®
PLEASE, ERROL SKIN!! LET'S LEAVE THIS SQUALID SLUM!!–MY RELATIVES ARE WAITING FOR US IN THE MANSION ON THE HILL!!
BETTER DO LIKE SHE SAYS, BOY!! SHE ALLUS HAS HAD A HORRIBLE TEMPER–NOT THET WE EVER SEEN HER BEFO' IN ALL OUR LIFES—
NO SENSE WASTIN' TIME WIF US!!–WE HAIN'T NO RELATIVES O' HER'N. WE HAIN'T GOOD 'NUFF!!
BEFORE I GO, MAY I KISS YOUR SWEET, SCRAWNY OLD CHEEK!!
FEEL FREE, STRANGER!!
KEERFUL O' THET PIPE, SON!! ALLUS SETS FIRE T' MAH WHISKERS!!
AT LAST!! MY ANCESTRAL HOME!!
THESE ARISTOCRATS!!–THEY'RE YOUR FAMILY?
I'M DELIGHTED TO MEET YOU, COLONEL YOKUM!!–
EN-CHANTED!!
??–("SO THASS ME!!")
MAY I PRESENT MY WIFE, MRS. PANSY YOKUM!!–
SIGH!!–EF AH WERE REALLY HIM, AN' YO' WERE REALLY HER–WE WOULDN'T BE TH' MIZZUBLE LI'L SLOBS WE IS, WOULD WE?")
SHOOSH!!
–AND THAT'S WHAT I SAID TO WINSTON CHURCHILL!!–A BIT FRANK, PERHAPS, BUT HE TOOK IT LIKE A MAN!!—
IT'S ONLY BECAUSE HE RESPECTS YOU SO, DEAR!!–AS JOHN FOSTER DULLES SAID ABOUT YOU, ONLY THE OTHER DAY---
I'M EXHAUSTED!! I THINK I'LL RETIRE—
DID WE LAY IT ON TOO HEAVILY, MA'M?
HE LAPPED IT UP!!–I'M AS GOOD AS MARRIED TO HIM!!
4-7
Tm. Reg. U. S. Pat. Off.—All rights reserved Copr. 1957 by United Feature Syndicate, Inc.
THE NEXT MORNING–
EEK!!
Al Capp
Dear Bessie: I truly love you—but your family is so far above me that I cannot drag you down, by marrying you. I come from people as humble as those flea-bitten hill-billies we first met.
Oh, if only they had been your family, we could have made such beautiful music together. Goodbye, forever—Errol Skin

17 COMICS

Sunday Mirror 15¢

NEW YORK, N. Y.   SUNDAY, APRIL 14, 1957

LI'L ABNER by Al Capp

LI'L ABNER
by AL CAPP ®

TH' SCRAGGS SNATCHED HONEST ABE!!—

KETCH HIM, PAPPY, DEAR!!

JUMP IN, CHILLUN!!—AN' AWAY WE GO!!

PLEASE DON'T HARM OUR CHILE!!

HAIN'T IT INJOYABLE, HEARIN' A YOKUM SCREAM WIF TERROR!!

IT'S MOOSIC TO A SCRAGG'S EARS!!

HAW!!

THEY'S GONNA KILL THET IGGORANT FURRINER!!

THEES DRIVER HAS ABOUT THE SAME EENTELLIGENCE AS A BOOL!!

Tm. Reg. U. S. Pat Off—All rights reserved
Copr. 1957 by United Feature Syndicate, Inc.

OL-AY! ZE MOMENT OF TRUTH!!

YO' SAVED OUR CHILE'S LIFE!!—AH'LL DO ANYTHING IN TH' WORLD FO' YO'!!

ANY-THEENG?

Y-YASSUH—BUT-GULP!!—H-HOW COME Y-YO' SUDDENLY GOT SUCH A SNEAKY LOOK IN YORE EYE?—

SNEAKY LOOK OR NOT, YO' DONE GIVE YORE WORD!!

TO BE CONTINUED

LI'L ABNER
by AL CAPP ®

YO' SAVED HONEST ABE'S LIFE, AN' AH'LL BE **PROUD** T'DO ANYTHING FO' YO'—ON ACCOUNT YO' IS TH' **WORLD'S BRAVEST MAN**!!

WRONG, AMIGO!! I **WAS** THE WORLD'S BRAVEST MAN—

ALL US TREMBOLINOS ARE THE WORLD'S BRAVEST MEN—

—FOR 25 YEARS—BUT **THEN,** ·SOB!!—IT'S **MURDER**!!

THASS MERELY A CUTE EXPRESHUN. **EXPLAIN** YORESELF!!—

EET EES THE **BITTER TRUTH**!!—EVERY TREMBOLINO HAS BEEN A **GREAT** BULLFIGHTER—

BUT, **EVERY 25 YEARS,** WHEN THEY CELEBRATE THE "FEAST OF GOOD LUCK," BY A BULLFIGHT, IN MADRID—A TREMBOLINO IS KILLED!!

MY FATHER—MY **GRAND**FATHER—HEES FATHER, BEFORE HEEM—**ALL** GOT ZE HORN ON THAT LOUSY GOOD LUCK DAY!!—

NEXT WEEK COMES **MY**-SHUDDER!!-GOOD LUCK DAY!!—BUT, THE GREAT NAME OF TREMBOLINO WILL BE **MUD**—FOR I WILL NOT BE THERE!!—

??—WHEN YO' RUMPLES YORE HAIR LIKE THET, YO' LOOKS **JEST** LIKE LI'L ABNER!!—

I DO?

SHORE YO' DO!!

ONE WEEK LATER

ALL OFF!! MADRID!!

GULP!—A PROMISE IS A PROMISE!!

WATCH EET, SENORS AN' SENORITAS!! ONE BOOL 'AS ESCAPE!!

79

LI'L ABNER
by AL CAPP ®

L'IL ABNER IS IN SPAIN

COME BACK HERE, BULL!! DON'T SKEER ALL THEM PORE FURRINERS!!

TSK! TSK!!—HE DON'T MEAN NO HARM!!—HE JEST WANTS T'SASHAY IN THAR, LIKE EV'RYONE DOES, NOW AN' THEN—

FEEL FREE.

?? WONDER WHAR ALL TH' PEOPLE WENT—

CHUCKLE!!—YO' IS MAH FRIEND, HUH?

—AN' NOW—SIGH!—AH GOTTA COMB MAH HAIR BACK, AN' PERTEND AH IS TREMBOLINO!!—HE SAVED MAH CHILE'S LIFE, SO TH' LEAST AH KIN DO IS DIE IN HIS PLACE—

TREMBOLINO 'AS RETURNED TO DIE!!

ALL TREMBOLINOS, FOR GENERATIONS, 'AVE BEEN KEELED IN THEES BOOL RING, ON THEES HOLIDAY—"THE FEAST OF GOOD LUCK"!!—EET EES A ROMANTIC TRADITIONE!!

MATADOR

("HERE COME TH' BULL W-WHUT'S G-GONNA KILL ME!!")

5-3

??—IT'S MAH FRIEND!!—

NO, TREMBOLINO!!—DON'T FACE THE BOOL UNARMED!!

DON'T WORRY, FOLKS!!

AH'S AS SAFE AS IF AH WAS IN MAH MAMMY'S ARMS!!—SAFER!!

DON'T EENSULT THE GREAT TREMBOLINO WEETH THEES TIRED BOOL!!—

ONE FRESH BOOL, COMING UP!!

VERMOUTH KARPANO

LI'L ABNER

After the Ball Was Over — by AL CAPP

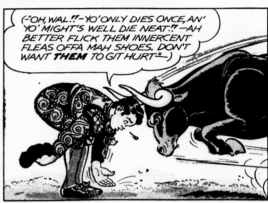

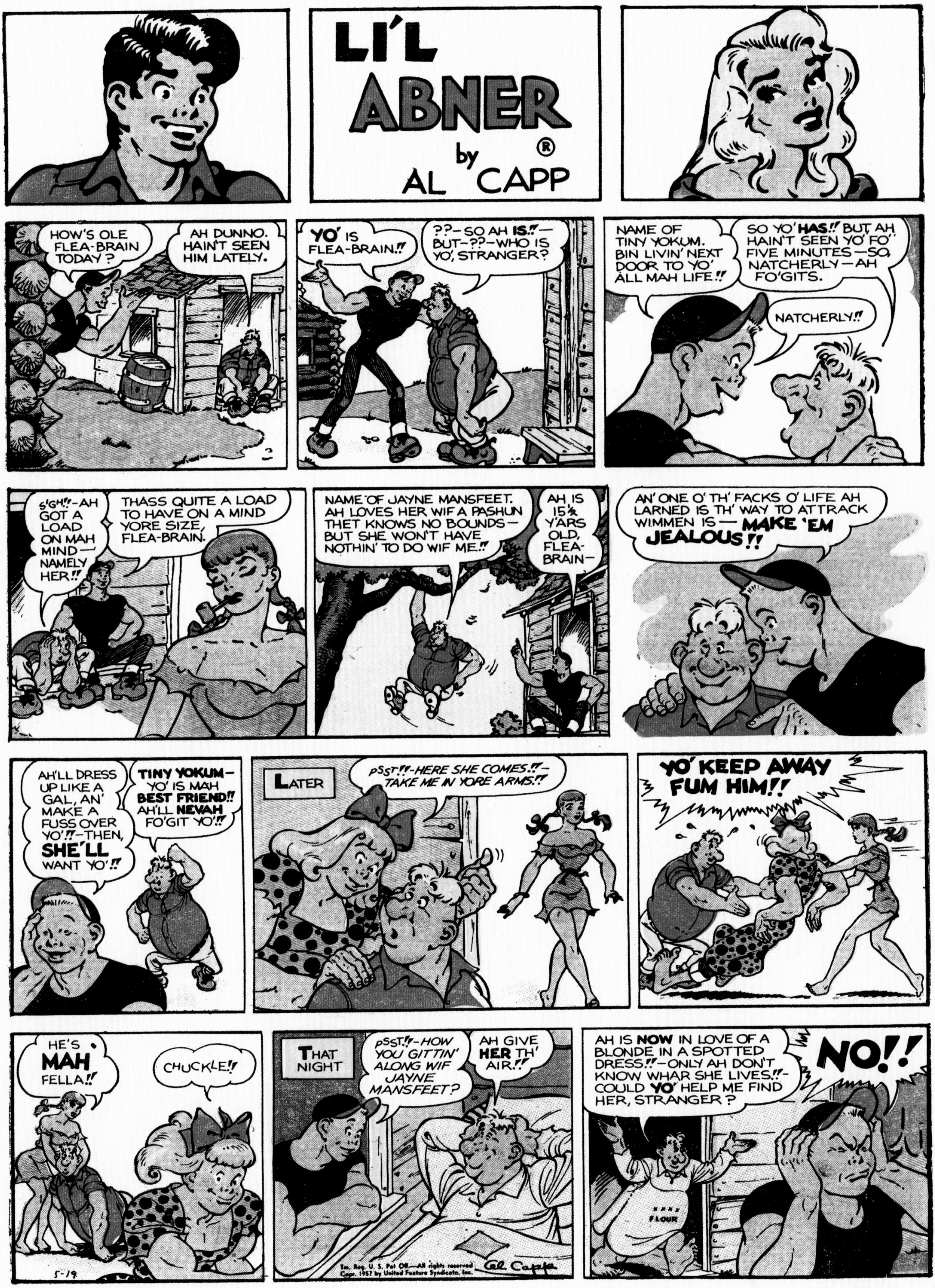
LI'L ABNER
by AL CAPP ®
HOW'S OLE FLEA-BRAIN TODAY?
AH DUNNO. HAIN'T SEEN HIM LATELY.
YO' IS FLEA-BRAIN.!!
??-SO AH IS.!!-BUT-??-WHO IS YO', STRANGER?
NAME OF TINY YOKUM. BIN LIVIN' NEXT DOOR TO YO' ALL MAH LIFE.!!
SO YO' HAS.!! BUT AH HAIN'T SEEN YO' FO' FIVE MINUTES-SO, NATCHERLY-AH FO'GITS.
NATCHERLY.!!
SIGH!!-AH GOT A LOAD ON MAH MIND-NAMELY HER!!
THASS QUITE A LOAD TO HAVE ON A MIND YORE SIZE, FLEA-BRAIN.
NAME OF JAYNE MANSFEET. AH LOVES HER WIF A PASHUN THET KNOWS NO BOUNDS-BUT SHE WON'T HAVE NOTHIN' TO DO WIF ME.!!
AH IS 15½ Y'ARS OLD, FLEA-BRAIN-
AN' ONE O' TH' FACKS O' LIFE AH LARNED IS TH' WAY TO ATTRACK WIMMEN IS-MAKE 'EM JEALOUS!!
AH'LL DRESS UP LIKE A GAL, AN' MAKE A FUSS OVER YO'!!-THEN, SHE'LL WANT YO'!!
TINY YOKUM-YO' IS MAH BEST FRIEND!! AH'LL NEVAH FO'GIT YO'!!
LATER
PSST!!-HERE SHE COMES.!!-TAKE ME IN YORE ARMS.!!
YO' KEEP AWAY FUM HIM!!
HE'S MAH FELLA!!
CHUCKLE!!
THAT NIGHT
PSST!!-HOW YOU GITTIN' ALONG WIF JAYNE MANSFEET?
AH GIVE HER TH' AIR.!!
AH IS NOW IN LOVE OF A BLONDE IN A SPOTTED DRESS.!!-ONLY AH DON'T KNOW WHAR SHE LIVES.!!-COULD YO' HELP ME FIND HER, STRANGER?
NO!!
FLOUR
5-19
Tm. Reg. U. S. Pat. Off.—All rights reserved
Copr. 1957 by United Feature Syndicate, Inc.
Al Capp

LI'L ABNER
by
AL CAPP ®

TONIGHT'S TH' TURNIP FESTIVAL DANCE, AN' AH IS —SOB!— BOYLESS, AGIN!!

YO' HAIN'T BOYLESS, BOYLESS. AH AXED FLEA-BRAIN T' TAKE YO'!!—

THEN AH IS STILL BOYLESS!!

WHUT AH LIKES 'BOUT FLEA-BRAIN IS, HE DON'T GIT SASSY WIF GALS!!

RIGHT!! THAR'S NO FUN GOIN' OUT WIF HIM!!—

HOWDY, FOLKS. AH HOPES YO' REMEMBERS ME—BECUZ AH DON'T—

YO' IS FLEA-BRAIN!!

DANGED EF AH HAIN'T!!

—YO' COME TO TAKE BOYLESS TO TH' DANCE!! BUT ONE THING YO' GOTTA PROMISE US— BRING HER HOME EARLY!!—

LOOKS MIGHTY GAY!!

SHOOSH!!—DON'T SAY NOTHIN'!! AH GOTTA REMEMBER SUMPTHIN'!!

OH, YES!!—AH PROMISED TO GIT YO' HOME EARLY!! LE'S GO!!

BUT, WE HAIN'T BIN TO TH' DANCE!!

AH DON'T RECALL NOTHIN' 'BOUT NO DANCE!!—CAIN'T KEEP MORE'N ONE THING ON MAH MIND AT A TIME!! HERE YO' IS—HOME EARLY!!

BUT, FLEA-BRAIN,

THIS HAIN'T MAH HOME!!

??—WHAT A LOVELY SURPRISE FOR A VACATIONING NEW YORK BACHELOR!!

I WAS THINKING OF GOING OVER TO THAT DANCE—-

COULD WE GO BY WAY OF "KISSIN' ROCK"?

ONE MONTH LATER —

PSST!!—TOMORRY NIGHT'S TH' TRASHBEAN FESTIVAL DANCE!!—OH, AH ALLUS DREADS TH' ARGYMINT SHE PUTS UP AGIN TH' ESCORT O' OUR CHOICE!!

ANOTHER DANCE— AN' AGIN AH IS BOYLESS!!

YO' HAIN'T BOYLESS, WE AXED FLEA-BRAIN TO TAKE YO'!!

NOW, HERE COMES TH' ARGYMINT!!

WHUT ARGYMINT? AH NEVER HAS A BETTER TIME THAN WHEN AH STARTS OFF WIF FLEA-BRAIN!!—

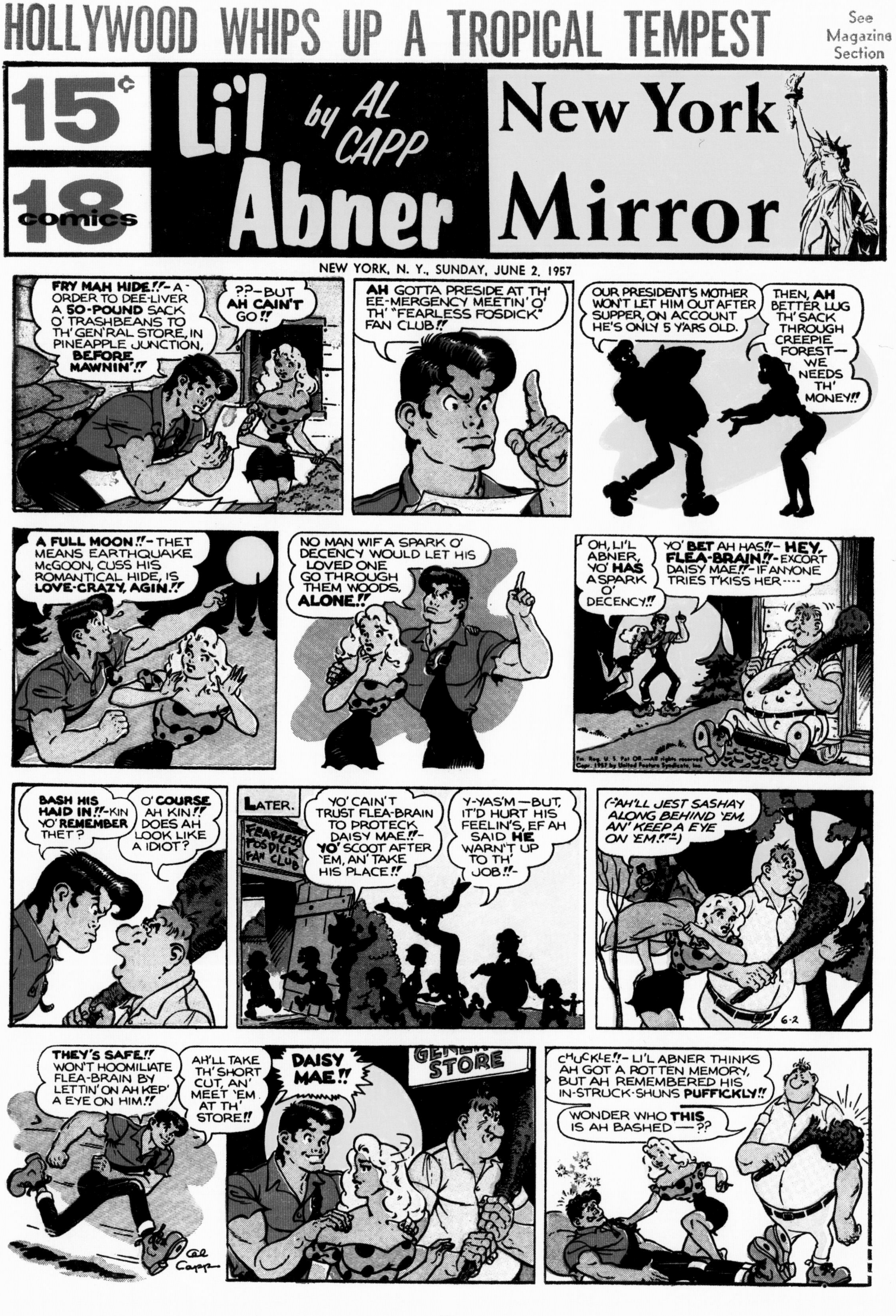
HOLLYWOOD WHIPS UP A TROPICAL TEMPEST
See Magazine Section
15¢
18 comics
Li'l Abner
by AL CAPP
New York Mirror
NEW YORK, N. Y., SUNDAY, JUNE 2, 1957
FRY MAH HIDE!!– A ORDER TO DEE-LIVER A 50-POUND SACK O' TRASHBEANS TO TH' GEN'RAL STORE, IN PINEAPPLE JUNCTION, BEFORE MAWNIN'!!
??–BUT AH CAIN'T GO!!
AH GOTTA PRESIDE AT TH' EE-MERGENCY MEETIN' O' TH' "FEARLESS FOSDICK" FAN CLUB!!
OUR PRESIDENT'S MOTHER WON'T LET HIM OUT AFTER SUPPER, ON ACCOUNT HE'S ONLY 5 Y'ARS OLD.
THEN, AH BETTER LUG TH' SACK THROUGH CREEPIE FOREST– WE NEEDS TH' MONEY!!
A FULL MOON!!– THET MEANS EARTHQUAKE McGOON, CUSS HIS ROMANTICAL HIDE, IS LOVE-CRAZY, AGIN!!
NO MAN WIF A SPARK O' DECENCY WOULD LET HIS LOVED ONE GO THROUGH THEM WOODS, ALONE!!
OH, LI'L ABNER, YO' HAS A SPARK O' DECENCY!!
YO' BET AH HAS!!– HEY, FLEA-BRAIN!!– EXCORT DAISY MAE!!– IF ANYONE TRIES T'KISS HER----
BASH HIS HAID IN!!– KIN YO' REMEMBER THET?
O' COURSE AH KIN!! DOES AH LOOK LIKE A IDIOT?
LATER.
FEARLESS FOSDICK FAN CLUB
YO' CAIN'T TRUST FLEA-BRAIN TO PROTECK DAISY MAE!!– YO' SCOOT AFTER 'EM, AN' TAKE HIS PLACE!!
Y-YAS'M –BUT, IT'D HURT HIS FEELIN'S, EF AH SAID HE WARN'T UP TO TH' JOB!!–
(–AH'LL JEST SASHAY ALONG BEHIND 'EM, AN' KEEP A EYE ON 'EM!!–)
6-2
THEY'S SAFE!! WON'T HOOMILIATE FLEA-BRAIN BY LETTIN' ON AH KEP' A EYE ON HIM!!
AH'LL TAKE TH' SHORT CUT, AN' MEET 'EM AT TH' STORE!!
DAISY MAE!!
GENERAL STORE
CHUCKLE!!– LI'L ABNER THINKS AH GOT A ROTTEN MEMORY, BUT AH REMEMBERED HIS IN-STRUCK-SHUNS PUFFICKLY!!
WONDER WHO THIS IS AH BASHED —??
Al Capp

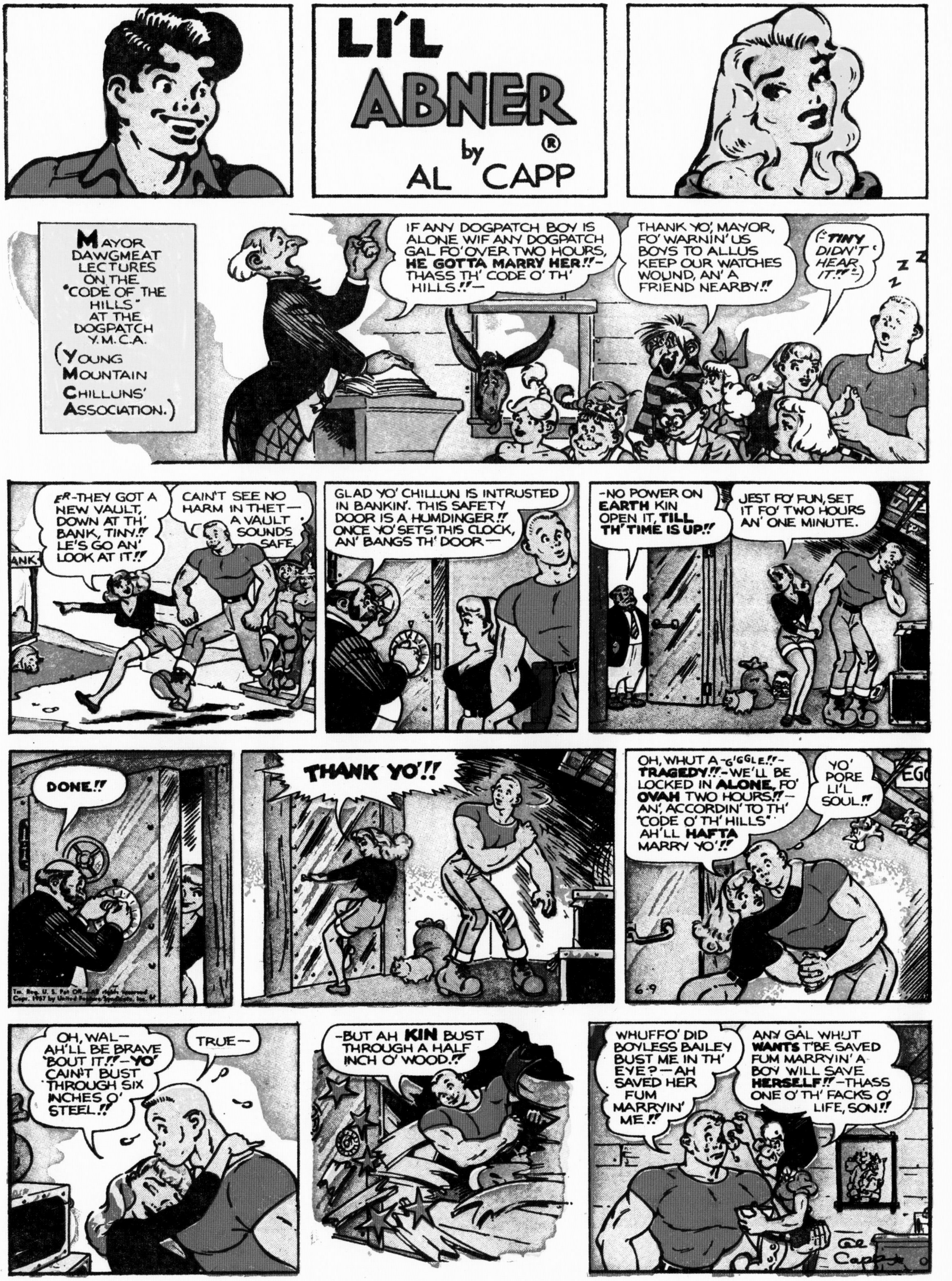
LI'L ABNER
by AL CAPP ®
MAYOR DAWGMEAT LECTURES ON THE "CODE OF THE HILLS" AT THE DOGPATCH Y.M.C.A. (YOUNG MOUNTAIN CHILLUNS' ASSOCIATION.)
IF ANY DOGPATCH BOY IS ALONE WIF ANY DOGPATCH GAL FO' OVER TWO HOURS, HE GOTTA MARRY HER!!— THASS TH' CODE O' TH' HILLS!!—
THANK YO', MAYOR, FO' WARNIN' US BOYS TO ALLUS KEEP OUR WATCHES WOUND, AN' A FRIEND NEARBY!!
(—TINY DIDN'T HEAR IT!!—)
Z Z Z
ER—THEY GOT A NEW VAULT, DOWN AT TH' BANK, TINY!! LE'S GO AN' LOOK AT IT!!
CAIN'T SEE NO HARM IN THET— A VAULT SOUNDS SAFE.
GLAD YO' CHILLUN IS INTRUSTED IN BANKIN'. THIS SAFETY DOOR IS A HUMDINGER!! ONCE YO' SETS THIS CLOCK, AN' BANGS TH' DOOR—
—NO POWER ON EARTH KIN OPEN IT, TILL TH' TIME IS UP!!
JEST FO' FUN, SET IT FO' TWO HOURS AN' ONE MINUTE.
DONE!!
THANK YO'!!
OH, WHUT A—giggle!!—TRAGEDY!!—WE'LL BE LOCKED IN ALONE, FO' OVAH TWO HOURS!!— AN', ACCORDIN' TO TH' "CODE O' TH' HILLS" AH'LL HAFTA MARRY YO'!!
YO' PORE LI'L SOUL!!
6-9
OH, WAL— AH'LL BE BRAVE 'BOUT IT!!—YO' CAIN'T BUST THROUGH SIX INCHES O' STEEL!!
TRUE—
—BUT AH KIN BUST THROUGH A HALF INCH O' WOOD!!
WHUFFO' DID BOYLESS BAILEY BUST ME IN TH' EYE?—AH SAVED HER FUM MARRYIN' ME!!
ANY GAL WHUT WANTS T'BE SAVED FUM MARRYIN' A BOY WILL SAVE HERSELF!!—THASS ONE O' TH' FACKS O' LIFE, SON!!
Al Capp

15¢ — 18 comics — Li'l Abner by AL CAPP — New York Mirror

NEW YORK, N. Y., SUNDAY, JUNE 16, 1957

LI'L ABNER
by
AL CAPP ®

PARIS!! – PEPE AND MIMI YOKUM AND THEIR DAUGHTER BABETTE, TO THE CINEMA GO.

MATINEE LES CINEMAUX AMERICAINS

FORMIDABLE!!

OO, LA!! LA!!

REGARDEZ LES SAUVAGES!!.

QUELLE HORRIBLE!!

IN ZAT SAVAGE COUNTRY WE 'AVE RELATIVES!!'– LES YOKUMS OF DOGPATCH!! NOW WE KNOW WHAT LIFE IS LIKE THERE!!

IN ZE SUBURBS, ZE INDIANS KILL EVERYBODY!! IN ZE CITY, ZE GANGSTAIRES KILL EVERYBODY ELSE!! WE HAVE FRANCS ENOUGH TO SAVE ONE!!

MAYBE THERE IS A CHILD!!

A BABY IN ZE HOUSE!! 'OW BORING!!

BABETTE!!– YOU WILL STAY HOME NIGHTS, AN' TAKE CARE OF ZAT BABY!!– YOU CANNOT EVERY NIGHT WIZ ZE BOYS GO!!

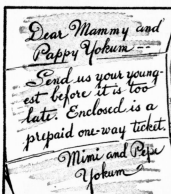

Dear Mammy and Pappy Yokum —

Send us your youngest before it is too late. Enclosed is a prepaid one-way ticket.

Mimi and Pepe Yokum

??–THIS TICKET'S NON-REFUNDABLE!! MEANIN' THEY CAIN'T GIT TH' MONEY BACK!!

THEN YO' GOTTA GO, TINY!! WE MUSTN'T BE NO EXPENSE TO OUR RELATIVES!!–

ZE BABY ARRIVES TODAY!!

I AM 15½ YEARS OLD!! A GROWN FRENCHWOMAN!! MAD!!–RECKLESS!! FULL OF FIRE!!

AN' ZEY WANT ME TO STAY IN, NIGHTS, WIZ A BABY?

NOT ME!!–

6-23

REGARDEZ LE BABY!!–

15¢ 18 comics

Li'l Abner by AL CAPP

New York Mirror

NEW YORK, N. Y., SUNDAY, JUNE 30, 1957

LI'L ABNER
by
AL CAPP ®

THE BRILLIANT YOUNG SENATOR SPEAKS—

WHAT **IS** "PROJECT P.U."??

IT'S COSTING US A MILLION A MONTH!!—

BUT NO ONE KNOWS **WHAT** IT IS!!— **I'M** GOING TO FIND OUT!!—

WOW!!— PROJECT P.U. MUST EMPLOY **THOUSANDS!!**

GASP!!— THIS MACHINERY MUST'VE COST **BILLIONS!!**

WHAT HAS P.U. ACCOMPLISHED?

THIS!!

IS IT AN INDIAN NUT?

DUN'T ITT IT!! IS THE TSICKRIT WEAPON WE'VE WORKED ON FOR 20 YEARS!!— COSTS **PILLIONS!!**

?? WHAT DOES IT DO?

EVERYTHING!! YOU KNOCK A HOLE IN ZUMBODY'S NOODLE— PUT **THAT** INSITE— SEW UP THE HOLE!!

YES—

THAT ZUMBODY CAN THEN READ ANYBODY'S MIND!!

A MENTAL RECEIVING SET!!

WE'LL KNOW WHAT THEY'RE THINKING IN THE KREMLIN!! WE'LL BE THE **SAFEST** NATION ON EARTH!!

HA!! BUT, IS ONE BROBLEM!!

WHO, IN ALL AMERICA, GOT A NOODLE **PATRIOTIC** ENOUGH, **PURE** ENOUGH, **VACANT** ENOUGH TO TRUST **THIS** INVENTION IN?

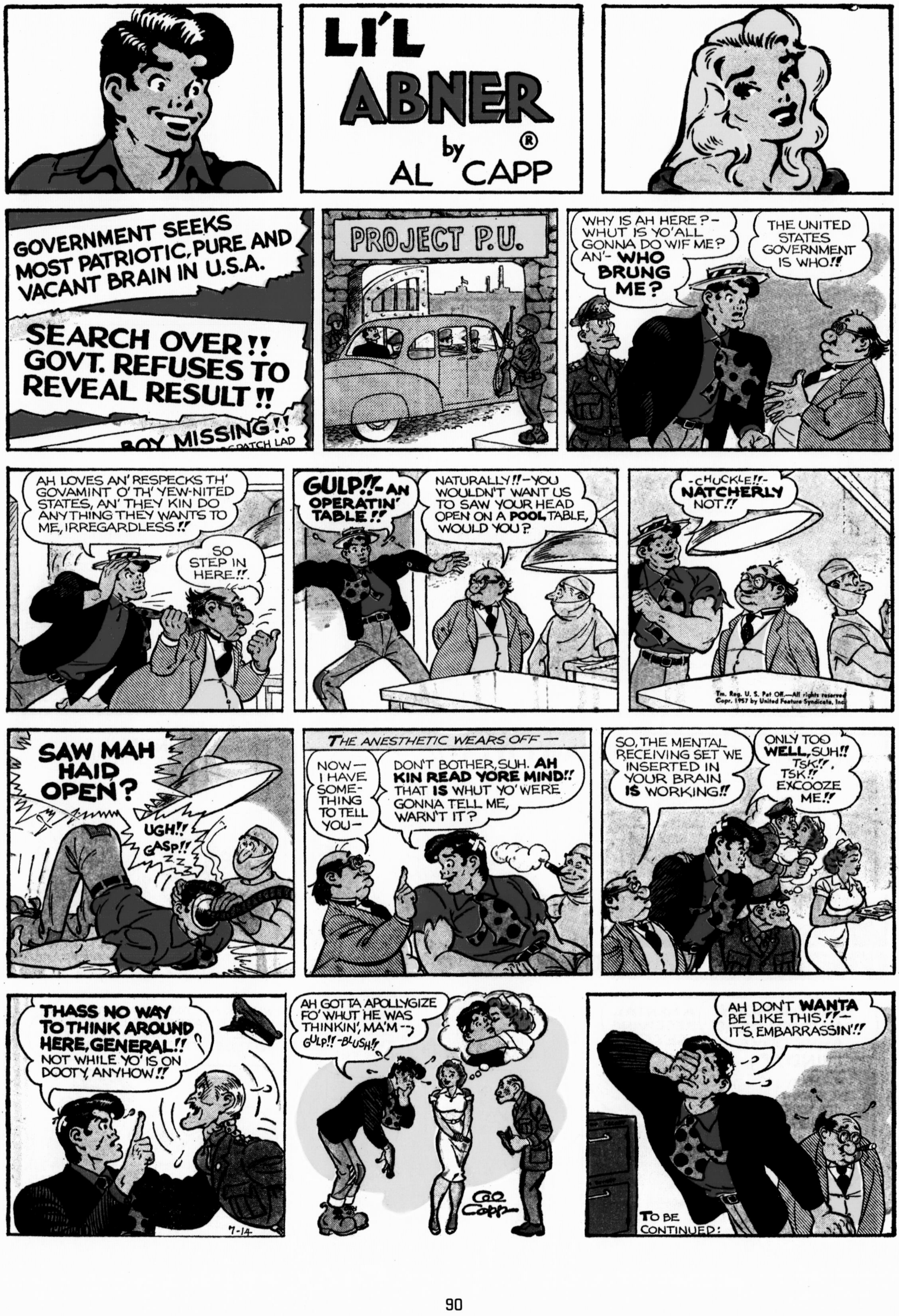
LI'L ABNER by AL CAPP ®
GOVERNMENT SEEKS MOST PATRIOTIC, PURE AND VACANT BRAIN IN U.S.A.
SEARCH OVER!! GOVT. REFUSES TO REVEAL RESULT!!
BOY MISSING!!
PROJECT P.U.
WHY IS AH HERE?– WHUT IS YO'ALL GONNA DO WIF ME? AN'– WHO BRUNG ME?
THE UNITED STATES GOVERNMENT IS WHO!!
AH LOVES AN' RESPECKS TH' GOVAMINT O' TH' YEW-NITED STATES, AN' THEY KIN DO ANYTHING THEY WANTS TO ME, IRREGARDLESS!!
SO STEP IN HERE!!
GULP!!– AN OPERATIN' TABLE!!
NATURALLY!!– YOU WOULDN'T WANT US TO SAW YOUR HEAD OPEN ON A POOL TABLE, WOULD YOU?
–CHUCKLE!!– NATCHERLY NOT!!
Tm. Reg. U. S. Pat Off.—All rights reserved Copr. 1957 by United Feature Syndicate, Inc.
SAW MAH HAID OPEN?
UGH!! GASP!! ZZZ
THE ANESTHETIC WEARS OFF –
NOW– I HAVE SOMETHING TO TELL YOU–
DON'T BOTHER, SUH. AH KIN READ YORE MIND!! THAT IS WHUT YO' WERE GONNA TELL ME, WARN'T IT?
SO, THE MENTAL RECEIVING SET WE INSERTED IN YOUR BRAIN IS WORKING!!
ONLY TOO WELL, SUH!! TSK!! TSK!! EXCOOZE ME!!
THASS NO WAY TO THINK AROUND HERE, GENERAL!! NOT WHILE YO' IS ON DOOTY, ANYHOW!!
7-14
AH GOTTA APOLLYGIZE FO' WHUT HE WAS THINKIN', MA'M–. GULP!!–BLUSH!!
Al Capp
AH DON'T WANTA BE LIKE THIS!!– IT'S EMBARRASSIN'!!
TO BE CONTINUED:

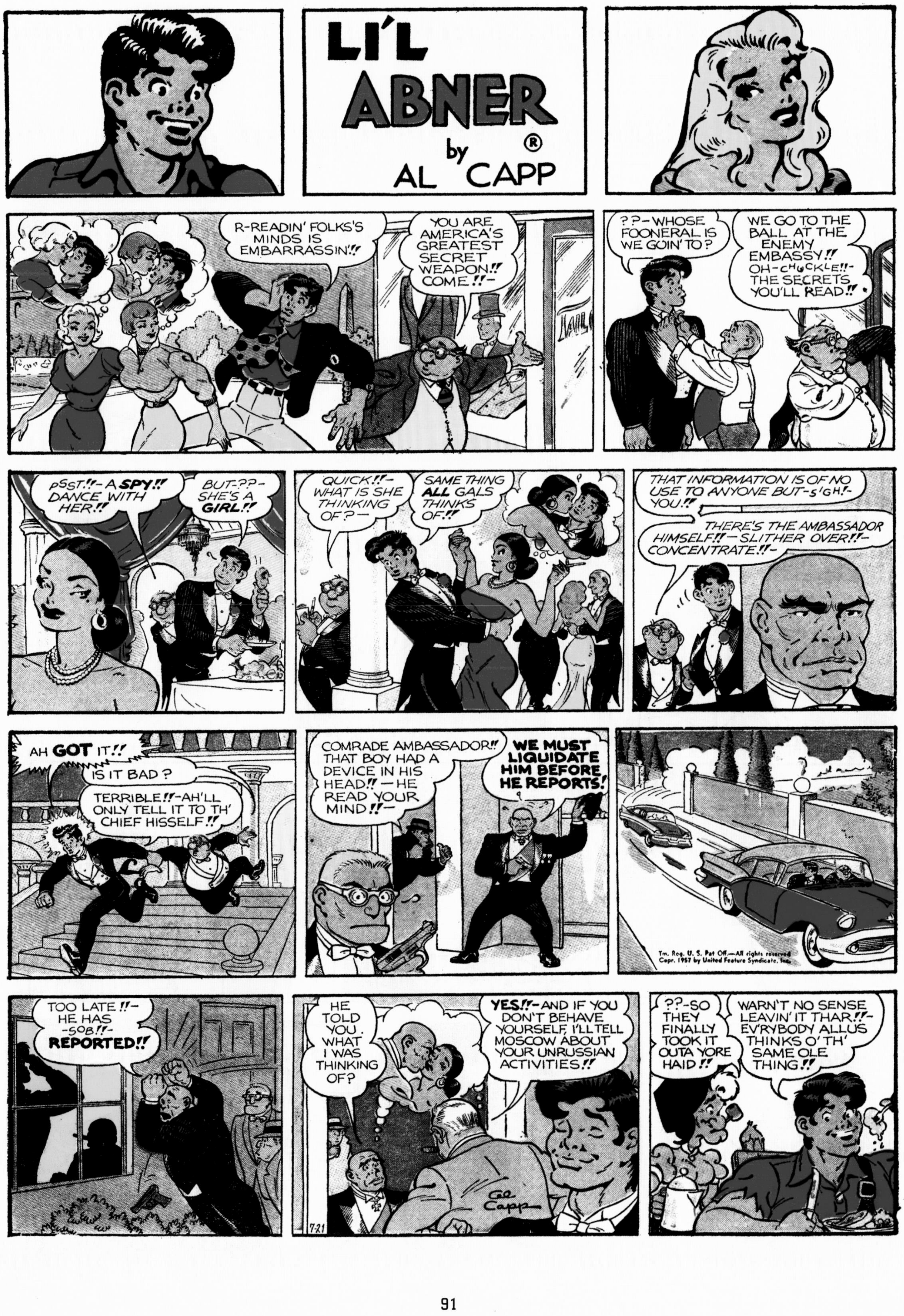
LI'L ABNER ® by AL CAPP
R-READIN' FOLKS'S MINDS IS EMBARRASSIN'!!
YOU ARE AMERICA'S GREATEST SECRET WEAPON!! COME!!-
??-WHOSE FOONERAL IS WE GOIN' TO?
WE GO TO THE BALL AT THE ENEMY EMBASSY!! OH-CHUCKLE!!-THE SECRETS YOU'LL READ!!
PSST!!-A SPY!! DANCE WITH HER!!
BUT-??-SHE'S A GIRL!!
QUICK!!-WHAT IS SHE THINKING OF?-
SAME THING ALL GALS THINKS OF!!
THAT INFORMATION IS OF NO USE TO ANYONE BUT-SIGH!-YOU!!
THERE'S THE AMBASSADOR HIMSELF!!-SLITHER OVER!!-CONCENTRATE!!-
AH GOT IT!!
IS IT BAD?
TERRIBLE!!-AH'LL ONLY TELL IT TO TH' CHIEF HISSELF!!
COMRADE AMBASSADOR!! THAT BOY HAD A DEVICE IN HIS HEAD!!-HE READ YOUR MIND!!-
WE MUST LIQUIDATE HIM BEFORE HE REPORTS!
Tm. Reg. U. S. Pat Off.—All rights reserved
Copr. 1957 by United Feature Syndicate, Inc.
TOO LATE!!-HE HAS-SOB!!-REPORTED!!
HE TOLD YOU. WHAT I WAS THINKING OF?
YES!!-AND IF YOU DON'T BEHAVE YOURSELF, I'LL TELL MOSCOW ABOUT YOUR UNRUSSIAN ACTIVITIES!!
7-21
Al Capp
??-SO THEY FINALLY TOOK IT OUTA YORE HAID!!
WARN'T NO SENSE LEAVIN' IT THAR!!-EV'RYBODY ALLUS THINKS O' TH' SAME OLE THING!!

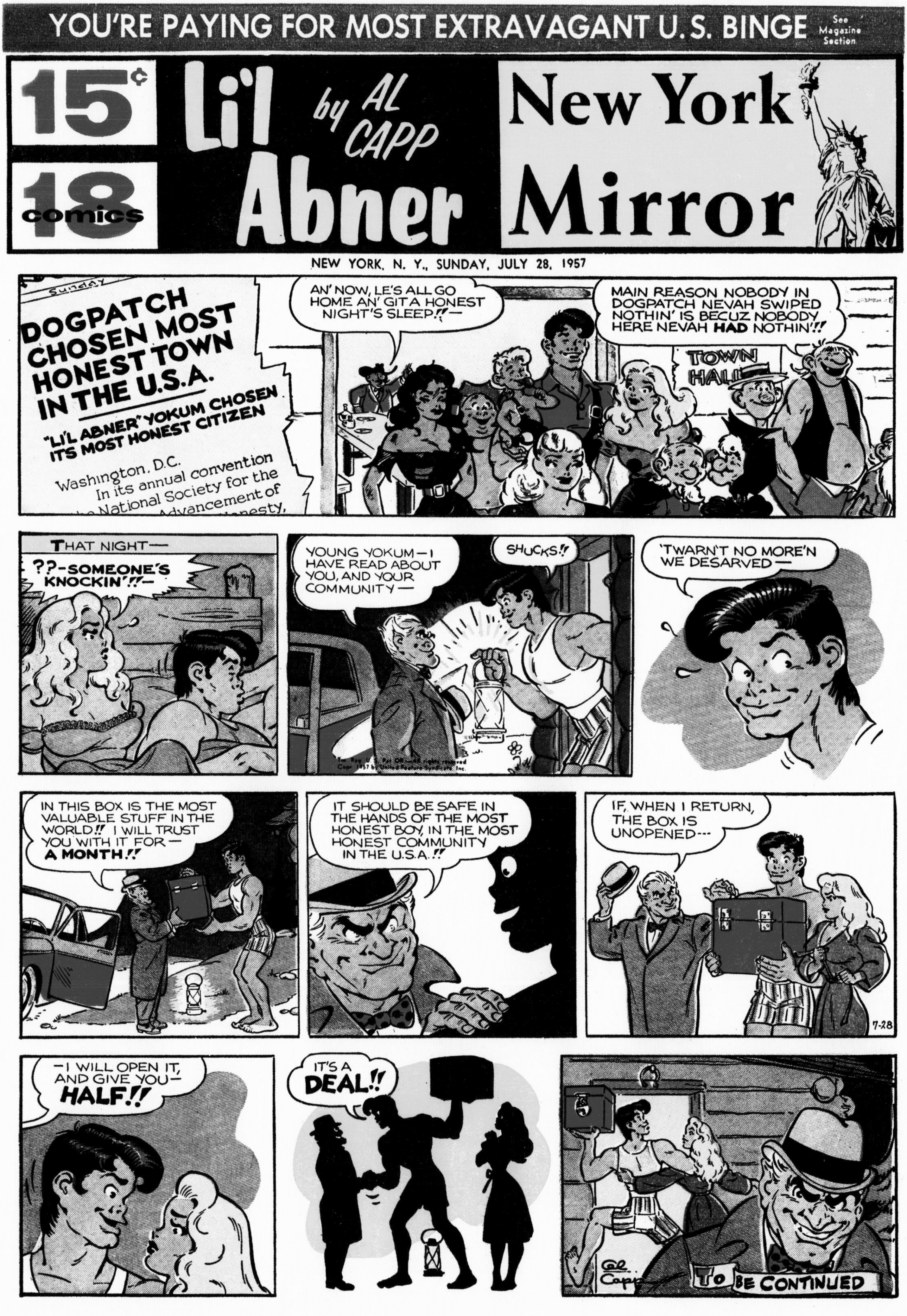
YOU'RE PAYING FOR MOST EXTRAVAGANT U.S. BINGE
See Magazine Section
15¢
18 comics
Li'l Abner by AL CAPP
New York Mirror
NEW YORK, N. Y., SUNDAY, JULY 28, 1957
Sunday
DOGPATCH CHOSEN MOST HONEST TOWN IN THE U.S.A.
"LI'L ABNER" YOKUM CHOSEN ITS MOST HONEST CITIZEN
Washington, D.C. In its annual convention the National Society for the Advancement of Honesty,
AN' NOW, LE'S ALL GO HOME AN' GIT A HONEST NIGHT'S SLEEP!!—
MAIN REASON NOBODY IN DOGPATCH NEVAH SWIPED NOTHIN' IS BECUZ NOBODY HERE NEVAH HAD NOTHIN'!!
TOWN HALL
THAT NIGHT—
??-SOMEONE'S KNOCKIN'!!—
YOUNG YOKUM—I HAVE READ ABOUT YOU, AND YOUR COMMUNITY—
SHUCKS!!
'TWARN'T NO MORE'N WE DESARVED—
IN THIS BOX IS THE MOST VALUABLE STUFF IN THE WORLD!! I WILL TRUST YOU WITH IT FOR—A MONTH!!
IT SHOULD BE SAFE IN THE HANDS OF THE MOST HONEST BOY, IN THE MOST HONEST COMMUNITY IN THE U.S.A.!!
IF, WHEN I RETURN, THE BOX IS UNOPENED---
7-28
—I WILL OPEN IT, AND GIVE YOU—HALF!!
IT'S A DEAL!!
Al Capp
TO BE CONTINUED

See Magazine Section

15¢ 18 comics **Li'l Abner** by AL CAPP

New York Mirror

NEW YORK, N. Y., SUNDAY, AUGUST 4, 1957

LI'L ABNER
by AL CAPP ®

A STRANGER TRUSTED LI'L ABNER WIF A BOX O' TH' MOST VALOOBLE STUFF IN TH' WORLD.!!

BECUZ DOGPATCH WON TH' AWARD AS TH' WORLD'S MOST **HONEST** COMMOONITY!!

BOP!

WHUT IS YO' HONEST FELLOW-DOGPATCHERS **UP** TO ?

ROBBERY!!—AS ANY FOOL KIN PLAINLY SEE!!

AH SEES!!—BUT-UGH!-NOBODY IN DOGPATCH NEVAH SWIPED NOTHIN' **BEFO'**!!

THET'S BECUZ THAR'S -UCH!!-NEVAH BIN ANYTHING IN DOGPATCH **WORTH** SWIPIN' BEFO'!!

LOOK!! TH' STRANGER!!—

CHUCKLE!!-THAT BOX PROVED THE HONESTY OF DOGPATCH **WAS** SLIGHTLY OVER-RATED!!

S'GH!!—HOW HEART-BREAKIN'LY TRUE!! BUT, **AH** KEPT IT SAFE AN' SOUND!!

SO, NOW OPEN IT, AN' GIVE LI'L ABNER HALF O' WHAT'S IN IT—**TH' MOST VALOOBLE STUFF IN TH' WORLD!!**

YOU CAN KEEP IT **ALL!!**

AIR!!-??

NATURALLY!!—THE MOST VALUABLE STUFF IN THE WORLD!!

94

LI'L ABNER
by
AL. CAPP ®

MARY WORM — America's most beloved old Busybody — by Allen FLOUNDER

Dear Mary Worm:
(America's Most Beloved Ole Busybody)
Just like the karacters in yore sweet sad comical stripp, ah has a problem only yo' cood solve. Oh, ah wisht yo' was reel an' cood meander to Dogpatch an' save our roont home!!
Yore heart broke reeder
Daisy Mae Yokum, D.W.
(deserted wife)

8-18

95

15¢ **18 comics** **Li'l Abner** by AL CAPP **New York Mirror**

NEW YORK, N. Y., SUNDAY, AUGUST 25, 1957

15¢ 18 comics Li'l Abner by AL CAPP New York Mirror

NEW YORK, N. Y., SUNDAY, SEPTEMBER 1, 1957

Li'L ABNER.

The Worm Turns!!— **by AL CAPP**

YES!!—I AM MILTON GONIFF, CREATOR OF "STEVE CANTOR".

MAH NAME IS "LI'L ABNER"—

AH BIN WORKIN' FO' CAPP ALL MAH LIFE—

—AN' LOOK AT ME!! STILL AS RAGGED AN' IGGORANT AS TH' DAY HE DREW MAH FUST BREATH!!

KIN YO' USE A HARD-WORKIN', EXPERIENCED COMICAL STRIP CHARACTER?

HMM!!—STEVE IS GOING OFF TO RISK HIS LIFE, TO SAVE CIVILIZATION!!

NOW, THASS TH' KINDA COMICAL STRIP AH WANTS T'WORK IN!!—WHAR FOLKS DOES SUMPTHIN' IMPAWTINT!!

Tm. Reg. U. S. Pat Off.—All rights reserved
Copt. 1957 by United Feature Syndicate, Inc.

HMM!!—THE VILLAIN IN THIS STORY IS SO DANGEROUS, STEVE WILL NEED A BODYGUARD!!

JEST LEMME AT THAT VILLAIN, MR. GONIFF!!—

STEVE CANTOR BY MILTON GONIFF

COLONEL CANTOR, YOUR ORDERS ARE TO CRASH IN CHINA—BEHIND THE IRON CURTAIN!!!

CRASH!!? J-JEST WHEN AH GOT THIS NEW SUIT!!

YOU WILL BE TAKEN PRISONER, TORTURED, STARVED AND DRUGGED!!

VERY GOOD SIR!

VERY GOOD?? IS YO' CRAZY?

YOU WILL THEN BE CONFRONTED BY THE U.S.A.'S MOST DANGEROUS ENEMY!!

NOW YO' IS TALKIN'! JEST LEMME AT THAT ENEMY!

IT WILL BE JEWEL BRYNNER, THE ONLY BALD GIRL SPY IN THE ORIENT!

WHUT A HAIR-RAISIN' SIGHT !!!—

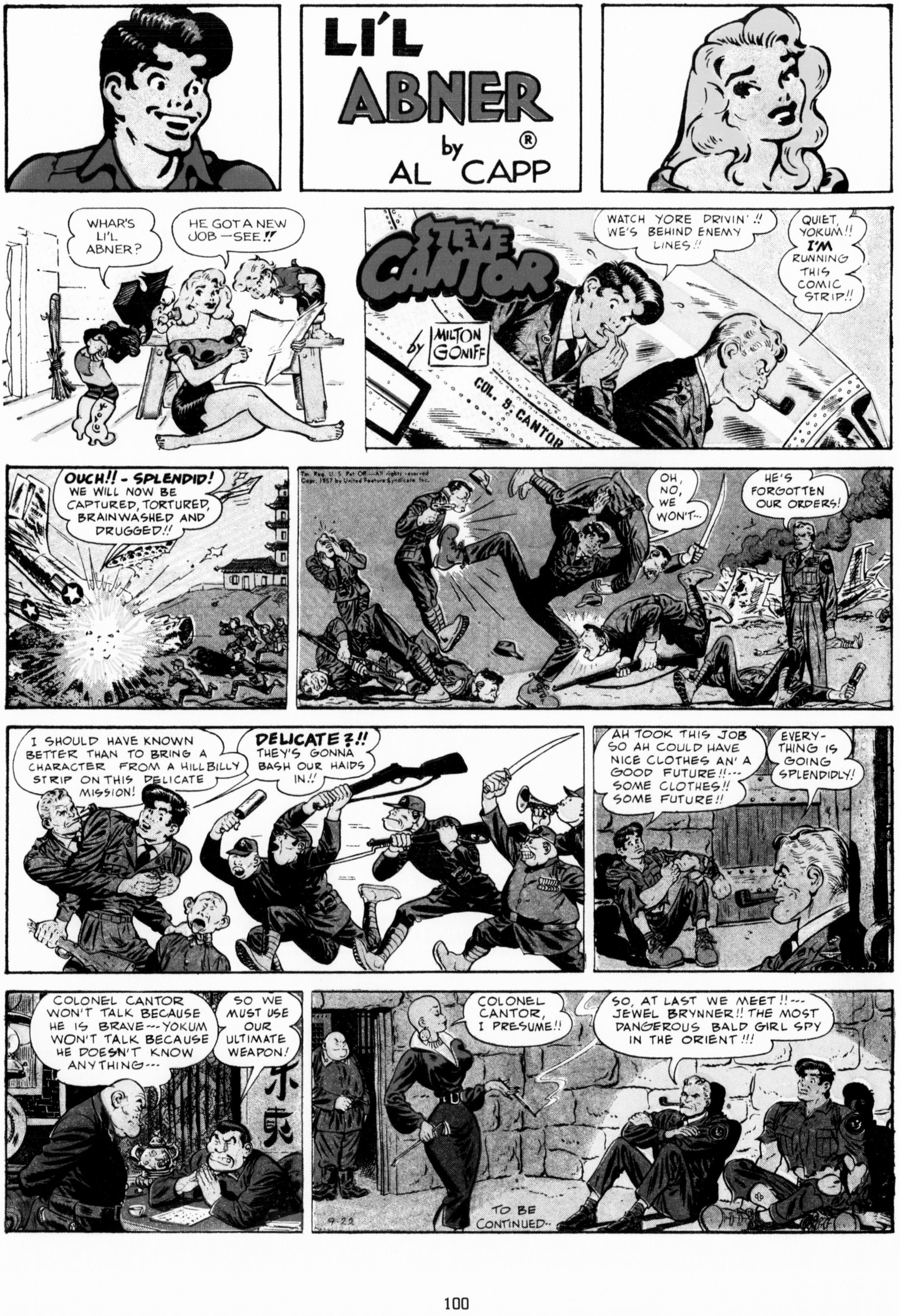
LI'L ABNER
by AL CAPP ®
WHAR'S LI'L ABNER?
HE GOT A NEW JOB —SEE!!
STEVE CANTOR
by MILTON GONIFF
WATCH YORE DRIVIN'!! WE'S BEHIND ENEMY LINES!!
QUIET, YOKUM!! I'M RUNNING THIS COMIC STRIP!!
COL. S. CANTOR
OUCH!! - SPLENDID! WE WILL NOW BE CAPTURED, TORTURED, BRAINWASHED AND DRUGGED!!
Tm. Reg. U.S. Pat. Off.—All rights reserved
Copr. 1957 by United Feature Syndicate, Inc.
OH, NO, WE WON'T...
HE'S FORGOTTEN OUR ORDERS!
I SHOULD HAVE KNOWN BETTER THAN TO BRING A CHARACTER FROM A HILLBILLY STRIP ON THIS DELICATE MISSION!
DELICATE?!! THEY'S GONNA BASH OUR HAIDS IN!!
AH TOOK THIS JOB SO AH COULD HAVE NICE CLOTHES AN' A GOOD FUTURE!!--- SOME CLOTHES!! SOME FUTURE!!
EVERYTHING IS GOING SPLENDIDLY!
COLONEL CANTOR WON'T TALK BECAUSE HE IS BRAVE---YOKUM WON'T TALK BECAUSE HE DOESN'T KNOW ANYTHING---
SO WE MUST USE OUR ULTIMATE WEAPON!
COLONEL CANTOR, I PRESUME!!
SO, AT LAST WE MEET!!--- JEWEL BRYNNER!! THE MOST DANGEROUS BALD GIRL SPY IN THE ORIENT!!!
9-22
TO BE CONTINUED--

YORE PAPPY GOT A JOB IN ANOTHER COMICAL STRIP, BUT -GASP!!-LOOK WHO HE'S MIXED UP WIF!!

JEWEL BRYNNER, MOST DANGEROUS BALD GIRL SPY IN THE ORIENT!!

HMPF!! GULP!!

THE "DANCE OF IRRESISTIBLE TEMPTATION" SETS YOUR BRAIN ON FIRE, EH, COL. CANTOR?

SPEAK!!

NEVER!! BUT I'M AFRAID YOKUM WILL CRACK!!

OH, DON'T WORRY 'BOUT ME!! ---ALL AH KIN THINK 'BOUT IS- SMACK!! DROOL! --- SOB!!!--- PO'K CHOPS!!

HA!!---THE WAY TO A MAN'S HEART IS THROUGH HIS STOMACH!!

SNIFF!! ---?? -- PO'K CHOPS!! AH CAIN'T STAND THIS!! AH'LL TALK!!

I UNDERSTAND YOU AMERICANS HAVE PERFECTED A NEW SECRET CHEMICAL!! TELL ME WHAT THE INGREDIENTS ARE?!

YES!! YES!!! AH'LL TELL YO'!!

9-29

ONE HOUR LATER---

I'VE MIXED IT!!---WHAT DO I DO NOW---?

RUB IT ON YORE HAID!!

FOOL!! THAT ISN'T THE FORMULA WE WERE AFTER!!

IT'S THE FORMULA I'VE BEEN AFTER--- ALL MY LIFE!!-

COME, BUDDIES--- OFF TO THE U.S.A.--- I WILL HELP MY REAL FRIENDS!!

AH'M GOIN' BACK TO MAH OLE JOB!! PO'K CHOPS IS TOO HARD T'COME BY IN THIS STRIP!!!

15¢ 16 comics **Li'l Abner** by AL CAPP **New York Mirror**

NEW YORK, N. Y., SUNDAY, OCTOBER 6 1957

15¢ 18 comics **Li'l Abner** by AL CAPP **New York Mirror**

NEW YORK, N.Y., SUNDAY, OCTOBER 13, 1957

NEW YORK, N. Y., SUNDAY, OCTOBER 20, 1957

15¢ · 18 comics · Li'l Abner · by AL CAPP · New York Mirror

NEW YORK, N. Y., SUNDAY, OCTOBER 27, 1957

105

15¢ Li'l Abner by AL CAPP — 18 comics

New York Mirror

NEW YORK, N. Y., SUNDAY, NOVEMBER 3, 1957

CORNBALL'S HURRICANE IS GONNA WALLOP DOGPATCH AGIN!!

ALWAYS STARTS BY BLOWIN' CORNBALL'S CABIN OFFA NOAH'S PEAK!!

—AN' THEN IT HOWLS ROUN' DOGPATCH— BUT NO PLACE ELSE—FO' 7 DAYS AN' 7 NIGHTS!!—

EV'RY LIVIN' THING IN DOGPATCH LOCKS THARSELFS IN, TILL IT'S OVER!!

AH GOTTA GIT THESE PRESARVED TURNIPS OVER TO PAPPY!! HE'S GONNA BE LOCKED IN FO' A WEEK—PORE, GREEDY LI'L SOUL!!

HURRY BACK!!

IT DONE STARTED!! THAR GO TH' CORNBALL CABIN AGIN!!—

—AN' THAR GO TH' CORNBALL FAMBLY AGIN!!

TOO LATE, SON!! YO'LL HAFTA STAY HERE TILL IT'S OVER!!

WAL, AH WON'T WORRY!! DAISY MAE GOT A WEEK'S SUPPLY O' FOOD—AN' THET NEW ROOF-BEAM, AH JEST PUT IN, WEIGHS A TON!!

SUDDENLY, DAISY'S CABIN IS HIT!!

Reg. U.S. Pat Off.—All rights reserved
Copr. 1957 by United Feature Syndicate, Inc.

TH' NEW BEAM'S COMIN' DOWN!!—

H-HOPE AH KIN LAST TH' FULL WEEK—BECUZ NOBODY'LL C-COME TILL THEN!!

ONE WEEK LATER—

WAL, HERE AH IS, SAFE AN' SOUND!! HOW IS YO', DAISY MAE?

T-TARD!! MIGHTY TARD!!

AHH!!—NOW, AH FEELS BETTER!!

BUT—YAK!! YAK!!—LOOKIT TH' WAY YO' LOOKS!!—YO' IS NOW AS BOW-LAIGED AS A BANTY ROOSTER!!

THIS TRAGEDY TO BE CONTINUED!

15¢ 18 comics Li'l Abner by AL CAPP New York Mirror

NEW YORK, N. Y., SUNDAY, NOVEMBER 10, 1957

WILL THIS DRESS RUIN DAISY MAE'S CHARACTER?

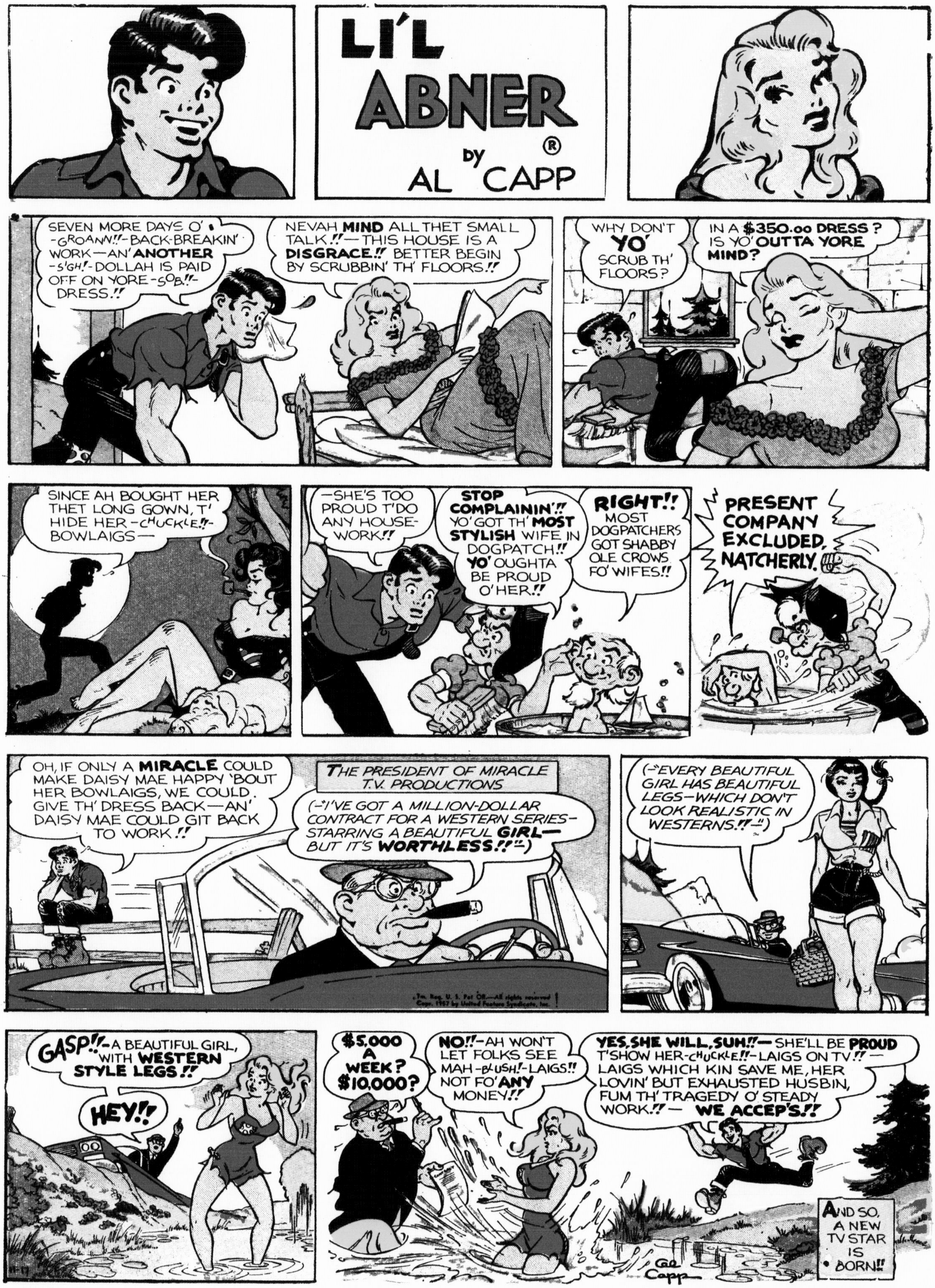
LI'L ABNER
by AL CAPP ®
SEVEN MORE DAYS O' -GROANN!!- BACK-BREAKIN' WORK—AN' ANOTHER -SIGH!- DOLLAH IS PAID OFF ON YORE -SOB!!- DRESS.!!
NEVAH MIND ALL THET SMALL TALK.!!—THIS HOUSE IS A DISGRACE.!! BETTER BEGIN BY SCRUBBIN' TH' FLOORS.!!
WHY DON'T YO' SCRUB TH' FLOORS?
IN A $350.00 DRESS? IS YO' OUTTA YORE MIND?
SINCE AH BOUGHT HER THET LONG GOWN, T' HIDE HER -CHUCKLE!!- BOWLAIGS—
—SHE'S TOO PROUD T'DO ANY HOUSE-WORK!!
STOP COMPLAININ'!! YO' GOT TH' MOST STYLISH WIFE IN DOGPATCH!! YO' OUGHTA BE PROUD O'HER!!
RIGHT!! MOST DOGPATCHERS GOT SHABBY OLE CROWS FO' WIFES!!
PRESENT COMPANY EXCLUDED, NATCHERLY.
OH, IF ONLY A MIRACLE COULD MAKE DAISY MAE HAPPY 'BOUT HER BOWLAIGS, WE COULD GIVE TH' DRESS BACK—AN' DAISY MAE COULD GIT BACK TO WORK.!!
THE PRESIDENT OF MIRACLE T.V. PRODUCTIONS
(—"I'VE GOT A MILLION-DOLLAR CONTRACT FOR A WESTERN SERIES—STARRING A BEAUTIFUL GIRL—BUT IT'S WORTHLESS!!"—)
(—"EVERY BEAUTIFUL GIRL HAS BEAUTIFUL LEGS—WHICH DON'T LOOK REALISTIC IN WESTERNS.!!"—)
GASP!!- A BEAUTIFUL GIRL, WITH WESTERN STYLE LEGS!!
HEY!!
$5,000 A WEEK? $10,000?
NO!!- AH WON'T LET FOLKS SEE MAH -BLUSH!- LAIGS!! NOT FO' ANY MONEY!!
YES, SHE WILL, SUH!!—SHE'LL BE PROUD T'SHOW HER -CHUCKLE!!- LAIGS ON TV!!—LAIGS WHICH KIN SAVE ME, HER LOVIN' BUT EXHAUSTED HUSBIN, FUM TH' TRAGEDY O' STEADY WORK.!!— WE ACCEP'S.!!
AND SO, A NEW TV STAR IS BORN!!
Al Capp

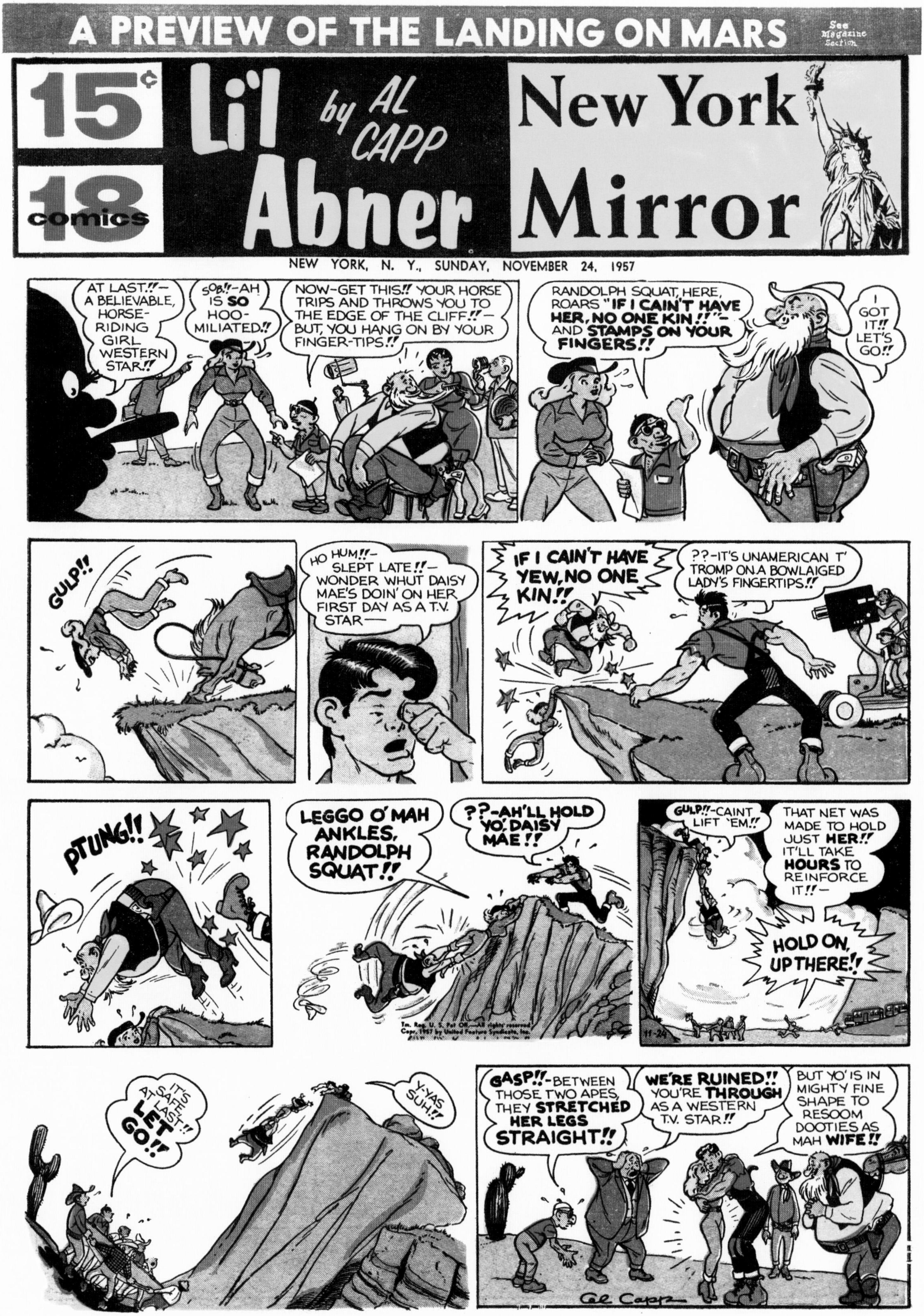

A PREVIEW OF THE LANDING ON MARS
See Magazine Section
15¢
18 comics
Li'l Abner
by AL CAPP
New York Mirror
NEW YORK, N. Y., SUNDAY, NOVEMBER 24, 1957
AT LAST!!— A BELIEVABLE, HORSE-RIDING GIRL WESTERN STAR!!
SOB!!—AH IS SO HOO-MILIATED!!
NOW—GET THIS!! YOUR HORSE TRIPS AND THROWS YOU TO THE EDGE OF THE CLIFF!!— BUT, YOU HANG ON BY YOUR FINGER-TIPS!!
RANDOLPH SQUAT, HERE, ROARS "IF I CAIN'T HAVE HER, NO ONE KIN!!"— AND STAMPS ON YOUR FINGERS!!
I GOT IT!! LET'S GO!!
GULP!!
HO HUM!!— SLEPT LATE!!— WONDER WHUT DAISY MAE'S DOIN' ON HER FIRST DAY AS A T.V. STAR—
IF I CAIN'T HAVE YEW, NO ONE KIN!!
??—IT'S UNAMERICAN T' TROMP ON A BOWLAIGED LADY'S FINGERTIPS!!
PTUNG!!
LEGGO O'MAH ANKLES, RANDOLPH SQUAT!!
??—AH'LL HOLD YO', DAISY MAE!!
Tm. Reg. U. S. Pat. Off.—All rights reserved Copr. 1957 by United Feature Syndicate, Inc.
GULP!!—CAINT LIFT 'EM!!
THAT NET WAS MADE TO HOLD JUST HER!! IT'LL TAKE HOURS TO REINFORCE IT!!—
HOLD ON, UP THERE!!
11-24
IT'S SAFE AT LAST!! LET GO!!
Y-YAS SUH!!
GASP!!—BETWEEN THOSE TWO APES, THEY STRETCHED HER LEGS STRAIGHT!!
WE'RE RUINED!! YOU'RE THROUGH AS A WESTERN T.V. STAR!!
BUT YO'IS IN MIGHTY FINE SHAPE TO RESOOM DOOTIES AS MAH WIFE!!
Al Capp

15¢ **Li'l Abner** _by_ **AL CAPP** **New York Mirror** 18 comics

NEW YORK, N. Y., SUNDAY, DECEMBER 1, 1957

LI'L ABNER
by
AL CAPP ®

TO BE CONTINUED.

15¢ **Li'l** by **AL CAPP** **Abner**

18 comics

New York Mirror

NEW YORK, N. Y., SUNDAY, DECEMBER 15, 1957

TO BE CONTINUED

112

15¢
18 comics

Li'l Abner by AL CAPP

New York Mirror

NEW YORK, N.Y., SUNDAY, DECEMBER 22, 1957

113

LI'L ABNER
by
AL CAPP ®

"AH'LL PUFFAWM TH' WEDDIN' CEREMONY WIFOUT **FACIN'** EITHER O' THEM —SHUDDER!! LI'L JINXES!!"

"JOE BTFSPLK WILL BE IN A PHONE BOOTH IN **WEST** PO'KCHOP—"

"MISS FORTUNE, IN A PHONE BOOTH IN **EAST** CORNBALL—"

"AN' **AH'LL** DO TH' MARRYIN', **SAFELY,** FUM TH' **DOGPATCH** PHONE BOOTH!!"

WEST PO'KCHOP

DOGPATCH

EAST CORNBALL

AND WHO WILL BE HANDLING THE CALLS? DAWN AMECHE, WORLD'S MOST CONFUSED TOLL OPERATOR.

MEANWHILE—IN N.Y., "LUCKY" LIPSCOMB, THE FABULOUSLY SUCCESSFUL GAMBLER, IS ABOUT TO PLACE A BET ON "I DO," IN THE FIFTH.

WHILE, AT THAT VERY MOMENT, IN CALIFORNIA, A TALENT SCOUT IS ABOUT TO AUDITION A TALKING MULE, BY PHONE, TO A GROUP OF T.V. EXECUTIVES IN NEW YORK—

NATURALLY, ALL THE CALLS COME IN AT THE SAME TIME.

YES!! YES!! "I DO!!" OF COURSE "I DO!!"

AH HEERD **SOME**ONE SAY "**AH DO!!"**—OH THIS IS TH' LUCKIEST MOMENT O' MAH LIFE!!

AND I DO, TOO!!

HEE HAW!! I DO!!

—AH PRONOUNCES TH' ENTIRE MESS MAN AN' WIFE!!—

LATER—THE TRAGEDY BECOMES CLEAR —

PALS!!—THE WIRES GOT **CROSSED!!**—I JUST MARRIED THAT FAMOUS JINX—**MISS FORTUNE.!!**

SHE'S FLYIN' TO ME—**TONIGHT!!**

WELL, I'M FLYIN' **FROM** YA, TONIGHT!!

YOU WAS A GOOD GUY WHILE YOUR LUCK HELD OUT, BOSS —BUT, NOW, YOU'RE T'ROO!!

IN HOLLYWOOD

??—THIS AIN'T A T.V. CONTRACT, DOROTHY— **YOU'RE MARRIED!!**

SO, WISH ME HAPPINESS, AND TELL ME TO WHOM.

WAL, THASS TH' WAY TH'—SOB.!!—COOKIE CRUMBLES!! AH WILL TRY TO BRING SUNSHINE INTO TH' LIFE O' LUCKY LIPSCOMB.!!

AH WONDER WHUT DOROTHY LOOKS LIKE. WONDER IF SHE'S MAH TYPE—

NEW YORK

HOLLYWOOD

Some readers may wonder why the episode titles cited (in quotes) at the start of each annotation entry do not appear on the actual Sunday strips. We have chosen to use the larger "tabloid" size Sundays in these reprint collections. Al Capp's hand-lettered episode titles (often with distinctive double exclamation points) appeared only on the horizontal "half-page" formats some subscribing newspapers utilized. We are including the official titles here for the sake of archival completeness and for the added insight or humor they may provide.

—D.K.

November 27, 1955. Page 5. **"Milton the Masked Man."** (1 of 6). The villainous Frogman from Saturn and the Moose-Man from the Moon are spoofs of the Hawkmen of Mongo, the Lizard Men, Lionmen, and other interplanetary species originating in **Alex Raymond's** "Flash Gordon" twenty

years earlier. **Milton the Masked Martian**, with a cape, red and blue costume with a chest letter, and super powers parodies **Superman**. The TV adaptation of the DC comic book character began airing in 1953 and, like **Milton**, was sponsored by a cereal company. Conveniently enough for the plot, **Tiny Yokum** is a dead ringer for **Milton**, which is no doubt yet another in-joke aimed at cartoonist **Milton Caniff** (the third such reference in five months). In a similar parody back in 1941, **Li'l Abner** was **The Flying Avenger**.

December 4, 1955. Page 6. **"Tiny Can Fly!"** (2 of 6). The premise of a levitating girl permits assistant **Frank Frazetta** to create a sexy pose that

would not otherwise be possible. Note **Capp's** pun on the small carnival tent sign: **Swami Riva's** assistant is **"Olman Riva."**

December 11, 1955. Page 7. **"Hungry Hero."** (3 of 6).

December 18, 1955. Page 8. **"The True Believer."** (4 of 6). Why are the **Brooklyn Dodgers** and **Bernard Baruch** being

compared to **Santa Claus**? A few weeks earlier (as **Capp** was preparing this Sunday) the **Brooklyn Dodgers** (a.k.a. the "Bums") won the World Series for the first time in their long existence. **Bernard Baruch** was a wealthy financier who served as a close advisor to several U.S. presidents (including FDR's "brain trust") while devot-

ing much of his energy to world peace. Evidently **Capp** regarded him, like Santa, as too good to be true. *Lime* magazine is *Time*. A "Li'l Abner" *Lime* parody three years earlier so pleased *Time* that their 12/22/52 issue reproduced excerpts of the strip and **James A. Linen** gushed about the magazine's long relationship with **Al Capp** in a full page "Letter From the Publisher."

December 25, 1955. Page 9. **"The Tennis Racketeer."** (5 of 6). Is the young girls' **Rosebud Academy** a completely innocent name or a naughty in-joke? "Rosebud" is the cryptic dying word of **Charles Foster Kane**—ostensibly the name of his childhood sled—in *Citizen Kane*, the acclaimed 1941 **Orson Welles** film. **Kane** is based on newspaper baron **William Randolph Hearst**, who did everything in his power to bury the movie, but not just because of how

he was portrayed. It evidently revealed an intimate secret. **Hearst** maintained a long relationship with actress **Marion Davies**, forty-three years his junior. Author and filmmaker **Kenneth Anger** maintains in *Hollywood Babylon II* that "rosebud" was the secret pet name **Hearst** gave to **Davies'** clitoris, information that she let slip to certain confidantes in indiscreet moments. *Citizen Kane* screenwriter **Herman Mankiewicz**, a guest at Hearst's palatial San Simeon estate, picked up the juicy tidbit and inserted it as a riddle in the film. **Anger's** revelation was not published till 1984, five years after **Al Capp's** death, so how could the "Li'l Abner" cartoonist have learned this intriguing secret by 1955? **Capp** was a good friend of a fellow womanizer, **Charlie Chaplin**, who—very dangerously— was a lover of **Davies** during her relationship with **Hearst**. A series of coincidences? Perhaps. But given **Capp's** long penchant

for inserting blue content in his strip, it is not necessarily a stretch.

January 1, 1956. Page 10. **"School Daze!!"** (6 of 6).

January 8, 1956. Page 11. **"There's No Place Like Home."** (1 of 1). By this point in time, **Frank Frazetta's** principle task as **Al Capp's** assistant was to pencil each

Sunday "Li'l Abner." But this week's episode, a loving homage to **Marilyn Monroe**, was penciled *and* inked by **Frazetta**. It is also, notably, the only "Li'l Abner" original in **Frazetta's** personal art collection.

January 15, 1956. Page 12. **"What Are You Groping For, Van Grope?"** (1 of 6). **Aunt Bessie (Hunks)**, the fabulously wealthy New York City socialite and serial widow, is—rather astonishingly—the sister of dirt-poor **Mammy Yokum (Pansy**

| 1934 | 1955 |

Hunks). Bessie, first introduced as **The Duchess of Bopshire**, appeared in the very first "Li'l Abner" story in August 1934. The mug shots shown here, from two decades apart, demonstrate that **Bessie** can obviously afford the best plastic surgery.

January 22, 1956. Page 13. **"Flesh and the Devils."** (2 of 6). When the exclusive Gourmet's Club demands that **Crawley Van Grope** produce "ecstacy sauce"—which can only be derived by reducing a *Hammus Alabammus* to a single delectable drop—to secure exclusive membership, longtime "Li'l

Abner" readers know what is coming next. The world's last *Hammus Alabammus* pig lives in Dogpatch as a member of the Yokum family. Her name is **Salomey**.

 January 29, 1956. Page 14. **"Pig o' My Heart."** (3 of 6). The title is a pun on the song "Peg o' My Heart."

February 5, 1956. Page 15. **"The Trail of th' Lonesome Swine."** (4 of 6). The title plays on an oft-made feuding hillbilly film, *The Trail of the Lonesome Pine*. It enjoyed three movie incarnations by 1936. **Al Capp** has said that one of the silent versions was an early inspiration for "Li'l Abner." The celebrities mentioned in this episode are typical of a common **Al Capp** rhythm. He will often name two or three famous or well-established personalities, then throw in a final name as a funny incongruity. Actor/director **Jose Ferrer**, actor **Tyrone Power**, and TV comedian **Jackie Gleason**

were all at the height of their careers in early 1956. **Henny Youngman**, a Borscht Belt comedian, was not at the same level of fame. For similar examples of this comic rhythm see the April 1 and April 15, 1956 Sundays.

February 12, 1956. Page 16. **"Love Rears Its Ugly Head."** (5 of 6). **Commodore George Dewey** commanded the U.S. fleet

 that captured the Spanish fleet in Manilla, making him a hero of the Spanish-American War in 1898. The point being that

the *Hammus Alabammus* is thought to have been extinct for nearly sixty years.

February 19, 1956. Page 17. **"Tigerina Brings Home the Bacon."** (6 of 6).

February 26, 1956. Page 18. Welcome (—Shudder!!—) Strangers!! (1 of 3).

March 4, 1956. Page 19. **"No Tender Trap."** (2 of 3). *The Tender Trap* was a play and then a 1955 film starring **Frank Sinatra** and **Debbie Reynolds**.

March 11, 1956. Page 20. **"The Eyes Have It!"** (3 of 3). The modern civil rights movement in America effectively began with **Rosa Parks'**  famous arrest in Montgomery, Alabama in December 1955 for refusing to give her bus seat to a white person. **Al Capp** would have conceived this "Li'l Abner" plot very shortly after that national incident, given his syndicate's lead time. By showing that "square-eyed" people are no different than other people, particularly in redneck Dogpatch, **Al Capp** was obviously doing his part to foster understanding, tolerance, and integration. This three-part story was slightly expanded and edited into a color educational comic book titled *Mammy Yokum and the Great Dogpatch Mystery*, issued by the **Anti-Defamation League of**

B'nai B'rith in 1956. In his foreword to the giveaway comic book, the organization's chairman **Henry Edward Schultz** said:

"Each age develops its own art forms and its own literary figures. The novel and the caricature, for instance, reached a high degree of development in 19th Century England. In the meantime, in this country, the humorous short story and essay—sometimes biting, sometimes folksy—made

literary history. But on both sides of the Atlantic, the literary figures of the day—**Dickens** and **Mark Twain** to name just two—were concerned with the evils of society and the need for reform. ...**Al Capp** is a direct lineal descendant of these two traditions, speaking to us in the idiom of the mid-Twentieth Century in a mid-Twentieth Century form—the cartoon novel. ...He too seeks to improve our manners and morals with his skillful literary scalpel and the acid of his clever drawing pen."

March 18, 1956. Page 21. **"Inside Lower Slobbovia."** (1 of 3). In May 1954 Lower Slobbovia brought us the truth-inspiring **Bald Iggle** (see Volume 1). Exactly two years later the otherwise barren wasteland exports another previously unknown creature, the **Mimiknik**, a bird that can mimic any voice. Once again, hapless baritone **Nelson Eddy** comes in for a ribbing. **Eddy** first recorded "Shortnin' Bread" in 1942, so it was already well out of fashion by 1956. But repeated playing would drive an individual from *any* generation or continent quite mad.

March 25, 1956. Page 22. **"Listen to the Mimiknik."** (2 of 3). The title refers to "Listen to the Mockingbird," an old western

folk song. Pop singer **Eddie Fisher**, "Jazz Singer" **Al Jolson**, and Wagnerian soprano **Helen Traubel** are meant to represent a diverse musical universe.

April 1, 1956. Page 23. **"Radio Rides Again!!"** (3 of 3). The title comes from the well-known tag line of a popular radio program: "A fiery horse with the speed of light, a cloud of dust and a hearty 'Hi-Yo Silver!' The Lone Ranger rides again!" But the underlying point of the title and the premise is that radio, long the king of broadcast media, is getting soundly clobbered in the 1950s by its rival, television. The varying sounds of **The Sextette from Lucia** (**Donizetti** opera), **The Inkspots**, **Eddie Cantor**, and the **McGuire Sisters** are all well regarded in 1956, but **Margaret Truman's** voice is tolerable only to her doting father, the ex-

President. In 1950, *Washington Post* music critic **Paul Hume** trashed a public performance by **Ms. Truman**. Her irate father fired off a letter to the critic saying in part, "I hope to meet you. When that happens you'll need a new nose, a lot of beefsteak for black eyes, and perhaps a supporter below!" **Harry Truman's** own amateurish piano playing takes a hit in this week's installment as well.

The humor in the "Today on Radio" list lies in the juxtaposition of contemporary recording stars like **Frank Sinatra** and stars of earlier generations alongside (obvious to 1956 readers) non singers.

Some names stand the test of time (**Enrico Caruso**, **Fats Waller**), while other performers, well known in their time, are obscure to many readers today. The **Andrews Sisters** and **McGuire Sisters** were popular singing trios of the 1940s and 1950s. The earlier **Duncan Sisters** (**Vivian** as **Eva** and **Rosetta**, cross-dressing as a man and in black face as **Topsy**) toured America for many years in their musical comedy version of *Uncle Tom's Cabin*. In contrast, the **Gish Sisters** (**Lillian** and **Dorothy**), were famous as pioneer actresses in silent films, and thus specifically *not* known for their voices. **Alma Gluck**, a century ago, was one of the world's best known female vocalists, but her last name is straight out of Dogpatch. [**Ed**] **Gallagher** and [**Al**] **Shean** were famous singing Vaudevillians but [**Roy**] **Cohn** and [**G. David**] **Schine** were the "odd couple" on **Joe McCarthy's** senate sub-committee. **Billy Jones** and **Ernie Hare** performed as "The Happiness Boys."

A very unlikely quartet performs "Rigoletto" to **Harry Truman's** accompaniment. **Nellie Melba** was an international singing star in the 1890s and early 1900s. Her image still appears on Australia's $100 bill. **Roy Rogers** was a singing cowboy on both the big and small screen. Singer **Julius LaRosa** made headlines in 1953 when he was fired on live TV by temperamental variety host **Arthur Godfrey**. **William Jennings Bryan**, the three-time presidential candidate who died following the

conclusion of the high profile Scopes Monkey trial in 1925, was a fiery orator, but not known to be able to carry a tune.

April 8, 1956. Page 24. **"A—Shudder!!— Star is Born."** (1 of 6). The title comes from the popular 1954 film. **Louella Parsons** and **Hedda Hopper** were powerful and feared Hollywood gossip columnists whose influential words could often make or break stars.

April 15, 1956. Page 25. **"California, Here She Comes!"** (2 of 6). It's unlikely that diminutive children's TV show host **Pinky Lee** could knock out heavyweight boxing champ **Rocky Marciano**, even though he retired (undefeated) in 1956. **G. David Schine**, scion of a hotel chain, is mentioned by **Capp** for the fourth time in less than a year. He was an unpaid consultant to **Senator Joseph McCarthy's** Sub-committee on Investigations. When Schine was drafted, **McCarthy's** right hand counsel and closeted homosexual **Roy Cohn** fought extraordinarily hard to get Schine a deferral, suggesting a gay relationship to some observers. That didn't make him any less attractive to **Nightmare Alice**.

April 22, 1956. Page 26. **"The Night Is Young and He's so Beautiful."** (3 of 6). Like the ill-fated couturier **Hernando Slideaway** before him (see the Sundays beginning 2/6/55), **Dig Muddley**, the Hollywood gossip columnist, makes a Faustian bargain with lovelorn **Nightmare Alice**. His "crazy" prediction that "gorgeous" pianist **Loverboynik** [**Liberace**] will perform the "world's most perfect piano playing" confirms that **Capp** thinks very little of **Liberace's** piano skills. Note that **Loverboynik** here is drawn as a close caricature of **Liberace**, while earlier parodies of the popular pianist bore little physical resemblance.

Al Capp once said that **Liberace** was the only celebrity who threatened to sue him. In a 1965 *Playboy* interview **Capp** recalled receiving "a telegram from a California lawyer claiming that my character **Loverboynik**, a delicious, dimpled darling of a piano player, resembled a client of his.

Actually I thought that was a hell of a thing for him to say about a client. ...Somehow *Time* magazine found out about the lawsuit—possibly because I tipped them off—and asked me what my defense would be. I said my defense would be that there was no resemblance whatsoever between **Loverboynik** and **Liberace**— because **Loverboynik** could play the piano rather decently. *Time* published that and I never heard from the lawyer again. I never heard **Liberace** again either, but that was just luck."

Actually **Capp** was not quite correct about that being his only celebrity lawsuit. At least one other celebrity, author **Margaret Mitchell**, sued him, in this case over a parody of her famous novel, *Gone With the Wind*. Capp's faulty memory in this instance may be due to the sting of a loss, which forced an unprecedented public retraction in "Li'l Abner."

April 29, 1956. Page 27. **"Nightmare Alice's Wonderland."** (4 of 6). Capp recycles a cheap joke about **Grace Kelly** and **Walt Kelly**, last seen 10/30/55, and used a third time on 6/10/55. Comedian **Henny Youngman** is the beneficiary of his second plug in two months. **Arturo Rumplestain**, the world's greatest piano player, is based on virtuoso **Artur Rubenstein**.

May 6, 1956. Page 28. **"Guys and Dolls."** (5 of 6). Yet another title is a pun on a contemporary film. **Rory McGoon**, "Hollywood's handsomest star," is **Rory Calhoun** (mentioned by his actual name just three weeks earlier). **Calhoun**, like **Al Capp** (see the 11/4/56 annotation), was the focus of a damaging cover story in the notorious *Confidential* magazine the previous year, and his film career never developed as it might have. **Piper Pincus** is loosely based on actress **Piper Laurie**. **Marjorie Strain**

is inspired by **Marjorie Main**, an older actress best known for playing irascible **Ma Kettle** in a decade-long string of *Ma and Pa Kettle* B-movies.

May 13, 1956. Page 29. **"Space Cadet."** (6 of 6). The earth satellite shooting marriage-shy **Dig Muddley** into space predates the

launch of Earth's first artificial satellite by nearly sixteen months. The USSR's **Sputnik** did not orbit until October 4, 1957, an event that jolted America into the space race. The vast majority of Americans did not even know what an artificial satellite was when this prescient strip first appeared in print.

May 20, 1956. Page 30. "Will Success Spoil Jack Rockheart?" (1 of 6). The title is taken from *Will Success Spoil Rock Hunter?*, a Broadway play and later a film.

May 27, 1956. Page 31. "When Better Grace Kellys are Made, He'll Make Them!" (2 of 6). The title is a play on the longtime advertising slogan, "When better cars are built, Buick will build them." The conniving "movie and aircraft tycoon" **Jack Rockheart Jr.** is inspired by America's first billionaire, **Howard Hughes Jr.** Before the public became morbidly transfixed by his later persona as America's strangest recluse in the 1970s, **Hughes** was best known in 1956 as a skirt-chasing movie mogul (RKO Studio) who was romantically linked to numerous stars, as well as a

fearless pilot turned aircraft tycoon (Trans-World Airlines). When TWA bought his airline shares in the late 1950s for $750,000,000, it made **Hughes** the richest man in the world.

June 3, 1956. Page 32. "The Vanishing Americans." (3 of 6).

June 10, 1956. Page 33. "A Star is Born." (4 of 6). The same film-inspired title is used twice in ten weeks. **Al Capp** engages in wordplay in the newspaper clipping. Besides **Grace Kelly**, the first names that starving actress **Daisy Mae** edges out for her Academy Award all end in **"Kelly."** They are: "Pogo" cartoonist **Walt Kelly**, dancer/choreographer **Gene Kelly**, comedienne **Patsy Kelly** (a regular panelist on **Al**

Capp's 1953 TV game show, *Anyone Can Win*), actor **Paul Kelly**, sad-faced clown **Emmett Kelly,** and 1920s flagpole-sitting champ **Shipwreck Kelly.**

June 17, 1956. Page 34. "Has Anybody Here Seen Kelly?" (5 of 6). "Has Anybody Here Seen Kelly (K, E, double L, Y)?" was a popular song in the 1920s. **Bonnie**

Prince Charlie of **Monte Carload** is a riff on **Prince Rainier** of **Monte Carlo** (Monaco), the actual prince that **Grace Kelly** wed in a highly publicized ceremony the media called "the wedding of the century" in April 1956. She never made another film after either the celebrated marriage or this "Li'l Abner" parody.

June 24, 1956. Page 35. "From Here to Eternity." (6 of 6). A title is again drawn from a high-profile film, this time the 1953

Frank Sinatra vehicle. Li'l Abner's sudden and improbable appearance as the prince in disguise is a more farfetched denouement than usual.

For the fourth time, **Jack Rockheart Jr.**, following his rejection by the famous actress, emphatically proclaims, **"Ha!! Who needs Grace Kelly?"** But could **Rockheart** be a mere stand-in? Is it **Al Capp** himself who is bitter about a real life rejection? **Grace Kelly** biographer **James Spada** claims that the actress privately auditioned for the part of **Daisy Mae** before the 1956 *Li'l Abner* musical launched. The "audition" was alone in **Al Capp's** New York office, where, she claimed, he came on very strong to her, and she fled. Given this incident, **Rockheart's** month-long blustering proclamations—*Who Needs Grace*

Kelly?—have a decided secondary context. They are most likely **Al Capp's** own very public last words to the actress who spurned his aggressive advances.

July 1, 1956. Page 36. "Mammy Knows Best." (1 of 3). This week's title is a play on the popular TV show, *Father Knows Best.* **Available Jones**, first introduced in 1942, is a pencil-nosed hustler whose ever-present motto is "I'll do anything—for

a price!" He serves as a convenient catalyst for any sort of plot twist **Al Capp** desires.

July 8, 1956. Page 37. "The Good Samaritan." (2 of 3).

July 15, 1956. Page 38. "The Education of Tiny Yokum." (3 of 3). Naïve **Tiny**, who obviously knows nothing about the opposite sex, receives the third of his **Mammy's** homilies on "th' facts o' life."

July 22, 1956. Page 39. "Mammy Conjures up a Wide-Screen Vision, in Dazzling Technicolor!!" (1 of 4). **Mammy Yokum** first "conjured a vision" in October 1934, within two months of the strip's inception. Her mystical powers remain undiminished throughout the strip's long history. "Wide screen" and "Technicolor" are among Hollywood's well-publicized efforts to glamorize its product and to counter the new media upstart, television. **Mammy's** adding of "stereophonic sound" was also a big deal in 1956. Experiments took place earlier but stereophonic sound was first practically added to movies in the late 1950s and stereo records were not marketed until 1958.

July 29, 1956. Page 40. "When Evil Eyes are Smiling." (2 of 4). The title comes from the old standard, "When Irish Eyes are Smiling."

August 5, 1956. Page 41. "The Whammy vs. Mammy." (3 of 4). **Evil-Eye Fleegle** periodically wreaks havoc in "Li'l Abner." A Brooklyn native, he is one of the few non-Dogpatch regulars in the vast cast. He was well-enough known to be a guest star in the

Fearless Fosdick TV puppet show in 1952. The **Evil-Eye Fleegle** puppet displayed state-of-the-art 1952 special effects: light bulbs dramatically lit when his eyes hurled whammies. A national audience also heard him speak in his trademark Brooklyn accent. **Evil-Eye** even had his own licensed merchandise in the 1950s. "Evil Eye Fleegle [sic] and his Triple Whammy" was an elaborate battery-powered plastic lapel pin in the shape of **Fleegle's** face. Its flashlight-size light bulb eye shot a whammy when a pull-string was yanked. **Fleegle's** destructive "whammy" is among **Al Capp's** invented words to enter the general lexicon. The "double-whammy," in particular, is a favorite of headline writers (see sample). **Evil-Eye's** reference

to "paralyzing th' gints last year" is baseball talk. In 1955 **Fleegle's** beloved **Brooklyn Dodgers** defeated the heavily favored **New York Giants** (th' gints) four straight times in the National League play-offs. His whammy may indeed have influenced the outcome of the series, but **Evil-Eye's** claim of singing the hair off Giant manager **Leo Durocher** is suspect. **Durocher** was already bald.

August 12, 1956. Page 42. **"Bye Bye Miss Bluebird."** (4 of 4). The song "Bye Bye Blackbird" is the origin of the title twist. **Mammy's** obstinate theory about **Evil-Eye Fleegle's** innate unhappiness prevails, natcherly. The sequence allows her an opportunity to expound a variant of her most famous adage: "Good is better than evil, because it's nicer!"

August 19, 1956. Page 43. **"Doom it May Concern."** (1 of 5).

August 26, 1956. Page 44. "Ah, Sweet Mystery of Death." (2 of 5). The title comes from an old standard

song, "Ah, Sweet Mystery of Life." Another variant is used December 29, 1957.

September 2, 1956. Page 45. "Two Hearts That Beat It as One." (3 of 5).

September 9, 1956. Page 46. "A Pappy's Life is Not an 'Appy One." (4 of 5).

September 16, 1956. Page 47. "A Fambly Member Dies." (5 of 5). **Nelson E. Yokum**, the dead bird, is yet another poke at singer **Nelson Eddy**.

September 23, 1956. Page 48. "Love, Your Magic Spell is Everywhere." (1 of 4). "Love, Your Magic Spell is Everywhere" was a hit tune for the **Ames Brothers** in 1954; big enough that **Capp** reworked it on December 23rd. Statuesque bar wrestler **Joan L. Sullivan's** name comes from heavyweight boxing champion (1882-92) **John L. Sullivan**.

September 30, 1956. Page 49. "Here Comes the Bride." (2 of 4).

October 7, 1956. Page 50. "Here Comes Li'l Abdul!!" (3 of 4).

October 14, 1956. Page 51. "Too Young to Go Steady." (4 of 4). **Tiny** diagnoses **Abdul the Indescribable's** problem as "curvature o' th' swine." More accurately, **Abdul** has his head up his ass.

October 21, 1956. Page 52. "The Prince and the Pauper." (1 of 4). Long before **Madonna** or **Sting** assumed a single word persona, there was **Dagmar**, an early 1950s TV personality. **Dagmar (Jennie Lewis)** was a buxom blonde who played it dumb for laughs. She is the inspiration for **Bagmar**, the exotic dancer **General Bullmoose** lusts after. In 1956, his $2 cigar is the symbol of a billionaire's lifestyle, dramatizing the effects of a half-century of inflation. **Bullmoose's** *"By Charlie Wilson!!"* exclamation references

industrialist **Charles E. Wilson**, who inspired **Bullmoose's** mantra (see 4/4/54 annotation in Volume 1 of this series). His *"By John Bricker!!"* aside names a fiery conservative senator from Ohio, another figure **Bullmoose** presumably admires. The third powerful name **Bullmoose** invokes is **Conrad Hilton**, whose hotel empire bore his name.

October 28, 1956. Page 53. "Stranger in Paradise." (2 of 4). As last week's title from **Mark Twain's** novel suggested, **General Bullmoose's** doppelganger pulls a *Trading Places* on the unsuspecting capitalist. This week's title comes from a hit 1954 song by **Tony Bennett**. As **Bullmoose** is beaten by

his own bodyguards, he invokes the name **Fulton Lewis, Jr.**, a pro-McCarthy radio broadcaster.

November 4, 1956. Page 54. "You'll Cry Tomorrow." (3 of 4). *I'll Cry Tomorrow* was a 1955 film adapting actress and screen-

writer **Lillian Roth's** autobiography. This week's in-joke must have given **Al Capp** particular satisfaction. Selling his tell-all article, "The Secret Lives and Loves of General Bullmoose," to *Trash* magazine is a reference to publisher **Robert Harrison's** *Confidential*, a controversial gossip magazine whose circulation reached 3 million in 1955. In 1953 *Confidential* ran a widely read exposé on **Al Capp** called "The Secret Sex Life of Li'l Abner." *Confidential* pictured some of the sexual imagery purportedly hidden in "Li'l Abner" and, among many other controversial things said, "millions of children [are] among [Capp's] total readership of approximately 40,000,000 readers.

Fortunately the children in his audience do not realize that if **Al Capp** drew on walls or back fences what he draws in some sequences of Dogpatch doin's he'd be hustled off to a psycho ward quicker than the average devotee of erotica could say, 'Fanny Hill.'" The exposé made **Capp** livid. Just as he thumbed his nose at **Grace Kelly** (see 6/24/56) and later humiliated gossip columnist **Dorothy Kilgallen** (see 3/12/61) he similarly counter-attacked *Confidential* using his most potent weapon: the panels of "Li'l Abner." Calling the source of that article *"Trash"* on his own turf is a particularly satisfying form of public revenge. **Capp** once said, "You can't draw a dog without making a comment on the state of dogs." Thus *Time* magazine becomes the innocuous *Lime*, but *Confidential* becomes the loathsome *Trash*.

November 11, 1956. Page 55. **"A Fool and His Partner are Soon Parted."** (4 of 4).

November 18, 1956. Page 56. **"Beauty and the Beast."** (1 of 3). The name **Chester Ghoul** is a sly reference to fellow cartoonist **Chester Gould**, creator of "Dick Tracy" (which **Al Capp** parodied for years via his strip-within-a-strip "Fearless Fosdick"). *Lime* magazine (*Time*) is back, last seen exactly eleven months earlier.

November 25, 1956. Page 57. **"Love's Neighbor Lost."** (2 of 3). **William Shakespeare** inspires this week's playful title. In the mid 1950s there was a success-ful TV show called *The Millionaire* in which a multibillionaire would give away a million dollars each week. A man in a suit (**Michael Anthony**), would deliver the check to an unsuspecting recipient, much like the start of this week's episode.

December 2, 1956. Page 58. **"Beast of Eden."** (3 of 3). *East of Eden* was a hit

film for **James Dean** in 1955. A good decade before **Al Capp's** politics became overtly conservative, one can see the incipient signs of his resentment against welfare freeloaders in this story.

December 9, 1956. Page 59. **"When McGoon Comes Over the Mountain."** (1 of 1). Zaftig singer **Kate Smith** was a

television fixture in the 1950s. One of her signature songs was "When the Moon Comes Over the Mountain." The moon astronaut with a distinct German accent, **Von Floogle**, is loosely based on the ex-Nazi scientist **Werner von Braun**, who first developed the A-5 and V-2 ballistic rockets that decimated London during World War II. Following the war, **von Braun** became a high profile American citizen and was heavily involved in America's space program, including the development of the Apollo Moon Flight project.

December 16, 1956. Page 60. **"The McSwine System."** (1 of 3).

December 23, 1956. Page 61. **"Love, Your Tragic Smell is Everywhere."** (2 of 3). The

Ames Brothers song, "Love, Your Magic Spell is Everywhere," inspires this olfactory variant. Once again **Al Capp** brings his characters home to Boston (his residence) and, once again, the typical Boston Brahmin bachelor is played by **Henry Cabbage Cod**. Capp uses this character name often, without regard to a consistent look. Compare, for example, the tall, blond, and attractive **Cod** in this sequence, to the short, nerdy, and bespectacled **Cod** seen in the 11/14, and 11/28/54 Sundays (Volume 1).

December 30, 1956. Page 62. **"McSwine, Women and Song."** (3 of 3). "Wine, Women and Song" is a **Johann Strauss** melody. The internal logic of "Li'l Abner" requires **Moonbeam** and **Moonshine McSwine**—

like all other traveling Dogpatchers—to return home after a devastating truth about big city life is revealed. This time Boston simply proves too "backward." Sometimes **Capp** uses the logic in reverse, as with **Marilyn Monroe's** temporary escape to Dogpatch (1/8/56), and the **Gloria Van Welbilt** "switcheroo" (beginning 11/7/54).

January 6, 1957. Page 63. **"Yes Sir, He's My Babysitter!!"** (1 of 4). This week's title is from the song, "Yes Sir, She's My Baby." **Yawn L. Sullivan** is another (see 9/23/56) variation on early boxing champ **John L. Sullivan's** name.

January 13, 1957. Page 64. **"Man and Superman."** (2 of 4). The title has nothing to do with **Clark Kent's** alter-ego. It's from a devilish 1903 play by **George Bernard Shaw**, which includes a major sequence in Hell. The hellish last panel of this Sunday episode must have sent shivers down the spine of many readers. The clear implication is that innocent little **Honest Abe** has been left alone with **Milton**... *the Molester*.

January 20, 1957. Page 65. "The Criminal Babysitter." (3 of 4). If there was any doubt last week, there can be none now. Even the strip's title pronounces that **Milton** is a "criminal" babysitter. And previously victimized parents warn **Abner** and **Daisy Mae** that **Milton** teaches "the worst of all possible crimes" only to *little boys*! In an era when pedophilia was not a common topic, this episode was getting downright creepy.

January 27, 1957. Page 66. "A Fate Worse Than Death." (4 of 4). To quickly dispel the dark foreboding of sexual deviancy in the two previous week's strips, **Al Capp** reveals **Milton** in the opening panel to be a mere...*ax*  *murderer*!? But no, it's *worse* than that! In fact, as the title denotes, it's "a fate worse than death." It turns out that **Milton** was teaching young **Honest Abe** the worst of all possible crimes in Dogpatch... a work ethic.

February 3, 1957. Page 67. "Watch that Bulganik." (1 of 3). Only last March **Lower Slobbovia** brought the civilized world another exotic bird, the **Mimiknik**. This time it's the swift-flying **Bulganik**.

February 10, 1957. Page 68. "Popular Bulganiks." (2 of 3). The title is a bad pun on the magazine *Popular Mechanics*. In case you haven't been slavishly reading earlier annotations, **General Bullmoose's** "BY Charlie Wilson!" exclamation is a reference to **Charles E. Wilson**. The former head of **General Motors**, five years earlier, famously stated, "What is good for the country is good for General Motors, and what is good for General Motors is good for the country." This proclamation inspired our favorite cartoon capitalist's motto, "What's good for **General Bullmoose** is good for everybody!"

February 17, 1957. Page 69. "Bye, Bye, Bulganik." (3 of 3). The title is another variation on the song "Bye Bye Blackbird." The **Bulganik** story is a variation of the folk

story, "The Emperor has no Clothes," but it is the pragmatic Emperor (**Bullmoose**) who eventually sees the light and the suckers who remain naked.

The unscrupulous **General Bullmoose**, who seems to own most everything, is revealed here as the sole owner of America's television networks. A few years earlier **Al Capp** railed against such a monopolistic possibility at a Boston lecture: "The air [television] should remain, like the press, the property of private enterprise. But, like the press, the air should be run in an American way. It mustn't, like Russian air, be the property of a small group. It should, like the American press, keep its influence a clean and unpurchasable influence. TV should remain a business, but a business as great in its dignity and honesty as it is in its influence, not a shabby, unprincipled racket that is willing to sell itself and us for 30 pieces of silver." Today Americans have far more TV channels to choose from. But as ownership of America's television industry, as well as its press, is increasingly concentrated into the hands of fewer and ever larger conglomerates, and as even hard "news" is increasingly purchased and politicized, **Capp's** warning fifty years ago is more chilling and on the mark than ever.

February 24, 1957. Page 70. "A Little Knowledge is a Dangerous Thing." (1 of 4). Successful entrepreneur **Al Capp** may have had a special motive to concoct a **General Jubilation T. Cornpone** adventure at this particular moment in time (drawn about six weeks prior to publication date). Dogpatch's revered Civil War "hero" just happened to be the subject of **Stubby (Marryin' Sam) Kaye's** show-stopping song in the **Li'l Abner** musical, which opened on Broadway November 15, 1956. The musical turned out to be a long-running hit, with 693 performances in New York City alone, but **Capp** couldn't know that just a month or two following the opening. He probably couldn't resist

indirectly plugging the production, while providing a context story for the otherwise obscure but suddenly more prominent character. The actual **Rajah of Hyderabad** ruled a principality in Colonial India.

March 3, 1957. Page 71. "Cornpone Rides Again!!" (2 of 4).

March 10, 1957. Page 72. "Inside General Cornpone." (3 of 4). Is Capp not so subtly

pointing out that **Li'l Abner** is a horse's ass in the opening panel?

March 17, 1957. Page 73. "Up in Ruthie's Room." (4 of 4). **Rocky Punchiano** is based on former heavyweight boxing champ **Rocky Marciano**. **Tennessee Bernie** is a play on **Tennessee Ernie Ford**, a singer and entertainer. For readers who

haven't already noticed, **Li'l Abner** has inherited his extraordinary boxing skills from his **Mammy**.

March 24, 1957. Page 74. "One Woman's Family." (1 of 3). We haven't seen much lately of bearded "ape" **Earthquake McGoon**, known in earlier strips as "th world's dirtiest wrassler." He is one of the few secondary characters to appear in both *Li'l Abner* movies (1940 and 1959). Here he makes only a cameo appearance as an unlikely suitor of **Mammy's** oft-married high society sister **Bessie Hunks**, last seen marrying **Crawley Von Grope** on 2/19/56. The higher-type man that **Bessie** now sets her sights on is **Errol Skinn**, whose name is a play on actor **Errol Flynn** but who is a caricature of the bald actor **Yul Brynner**.

March 31, 1957. Page 75. **"Cabin in th' Sty."** (2 of 3). The title pimps the MGM musical *Cabin in the Sky*. **Al Capp's** self-casting of actual actors to play his hillbilly clan is a bit ironic. The successful Broadway musical *Li'l Abner* will soon be adapted as a Paramount film (released in 1959). Aristocratic actor **Sir Laurence Olivier** fits **Bessie's** devious purposes but is, of course, completely miscast as the actual **Pappy Yokum**. **Katherine Cornell**, a dignified stage actress, likewise would not have been an actual candidate for **Mammy**. However **Rock Hudson** in 1957 was a beefy, handsome actor who could have pulled off **Li'l Abner**. And, as **Capp** and his readers already knew, **Edie Adams** was already playing **Daisy Mae** on stage in 1957 (and winning a Tony award for her limited role) but, interestingly, **Adams** was the only major stage player to be replaced (by **Leslie Parrish**) in the Hollywood version. It is no doubt a coincidence, but **Adams** reports in her autobiography that **Capp** made a clumsy and unsuccessful pass at her while she was very publicly married to comedian **Ernie Kovacs**.

April 7, 1957. Page 76. **"The Letter Edged in Brrrack!!"** (3 of 3). The tearful folk song, "Letter Edged in Black," goes back to the 1890s. **John Foster Dulles** was the dour Secretary of State in the **Eisenhower** administration.

April 14, 1957. Page 77. **"Mammy Knows Best."** (1 of 1). The same title was used in 7/1/56. That similar episode first introduced **Boyless Bailey** and addressed a

similar theme, in which **Mammy Yokum** begins teaching the facks o' life to her naïve fifteen and a half year-old (though seven-feet-tall) son.

April 21, 1957. Page 78. **"Stranger in Paradise."** (1 of 4). **Al Capp** used the same title, based on a popular **Tony Bennett** song, on 10/28/56. The bloodthirsty **Scraggs** are avowed enemies of the

Yokums, going back to the very first year of "Li'l Abner" (1934). Clan patriarch **Romeo Scragg** and his sons **Luke** and **Lem** have one principle objective in life: to kill **Yokums**. Even kinfolk **Daisy Mae Scragg**, by marrying into the **Yokum** clan in 1952, and her son **Honest Abe**, are clearly regarded as part of the enemy.

April 28, 1957. Page 79. **"Gullible's Travels."** (2 of 4). The title parodies **Jonathan Swift's** novel, *Gulliver's Travels*. **Al Capp** was often compared to the satirist **Swift**, who also used a sharp pen and sometimes went to extremes to get his point across.

May 5, 1957. Page 80. **"This is a Lot of Bull."** (3 of 4).

May 12, 1957. Page 81. **"After the Ball Was Over."** (4 of 4).

May 19, 1957. Page 82. **"Love Song of the Flea."** (1 of 3). The name of **Jayne Mansfeet**, the object of **Flea-Brain's** momentary affection, is inspired by sexpot actress **Jayne Mansfield**. After four episodes featuring **Mammy's** sage advice on the opposite sex, **Tiny Yokum** is finally able to pass on some "facks o' life" to a fellow even dumber than he is.

May 26, 1957. Page 83. **"Don't Knock the Rock-Head."** (2 of 3). Today it would be unthinkable for a nationally syndicated comic strip to make fun of a developmentally disabled person (even **Bill Griffith's** ostensibly retarded **Zippy the Pinhead** speaks in intellectual non sequiturs). But in 1957, sorry **Flea-Brain** was fair game. Younger readers may need to be told that **Boyless Bailey's** phrase, "Looks mighty gay!" has no homosexual overtones. In 1957 it simply meant, "Looks like a lot of fun!"

June 2, 1957. Page 84. **"Slug Thy Neighbor."** (3 of 3). **Flea-Brain** is again the obvious idiot in the episode. But not even **Al Capp's** own readership is safe

from his satirical barbs. By revealing that **Li'l Abner**, himself no Rhodes scholar, is the only adult in the **Fearless Fosdick Fan Club**, and by noting that the club's president is five years old, **Capp** is slyly poking fun at all adults who are reading comic strips.

June 9, 1957. Page 85. **"Break the Bank!"** (1 of 1). The venerable "Code o' th' Hills" is evidently a fairly malleable legal concept. As recently as December 31, 1956, simply holding **Moonbeam McSwine's** hands invoked a marital obligation on **Henry**

Cabbage Cod's part. In the July 3, 1955 Sunday, **Tiny Yokum's** perceived kissing of **Stardust Trash** kicked in the Code o' th' Hills. And in this episode, **Mayor Dawgmeat** declares that "two hours alone wif any Dogpatch gal" is enough to invoke the Code. Thankfully Dogpatch is too poor to afford lawyers to sort it all out. This episode turns out to be yet another "facks o' life" lesson for **Tiny**.

June 16, 1957. Page 86. **"Handcuffs Across the Sea."** (1 of 1). "Hands Across the Sea" is a famous **John Phillip Sousa** march. Over the years, **Al Capp** made England a home away from home, spending a good deal of time at the Savoy Hotel in London. It was inevitable that he would playfully inject some British idioms in a Dogpatch context.

June 23, 1957. Page 87. **"Oui, M'sieu', C'est Mon Bêbe!!"** (1 of 2). After a poke at

the British, the French take a turn. Even the title this week is a translation of the

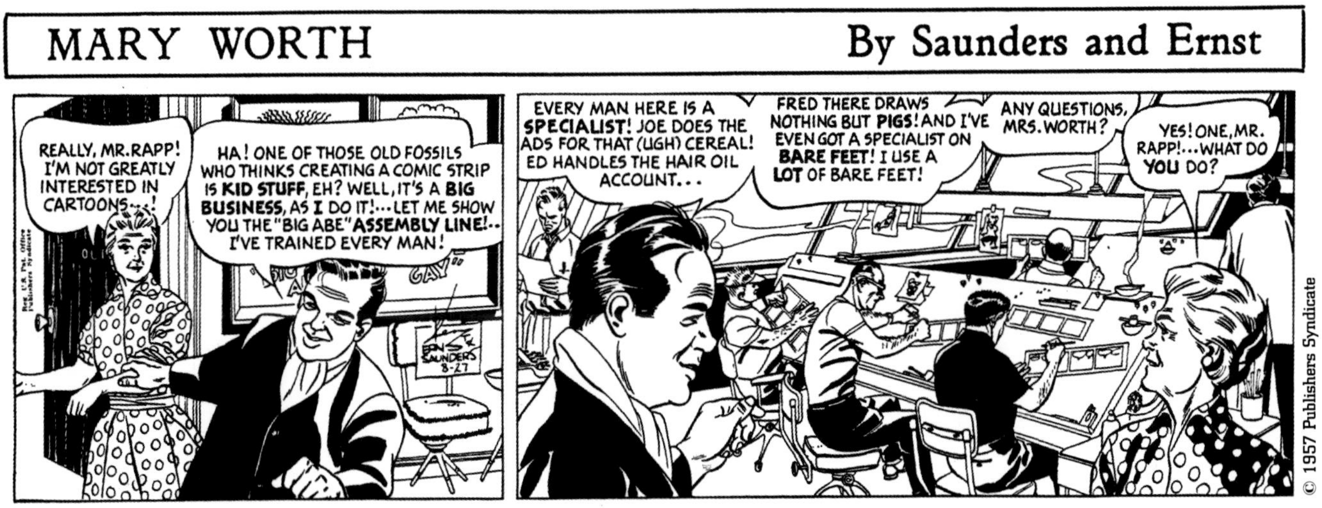
MARY WORTH
By Saunders and Ernst
REALLY, MR. RAPP! I'M NOT GREATLY INTERESTED IN CARTOONS...!
HA! ONE OF THOSE OLD FOSSILS WHO THINKS CREATING A COMIC STRIP IS KID STUFF, EH? WELL, IT'S A BIG BUSINESS, AS I DO IT!...LET ME SHOW YOU THE "BIG ABE" ASSEMBLY LINE!.. I'VE TRAINED EVERY MAN!
EVERY MAN HERE IS A SPECIALIST! JOE DOES THE ADS FOR THAT (UGH) CEREAL! ED HANDLES THE HAIR OIL ACCOUNT...
FRED THERE DRAWS NOTHING BUT PIGS! AND I'VE EVEN GOT A SPECIALIST ON BARE FEET! I USE A LOT OF BARE FEET!
ANY QUESTIONS, MRS. WORTH?
YES! ONE, MR. RAPP!...WHAT DO YOU DO?

© 1957 Publishers Syndicate

This August 27, 1957 "Mary Worth" daily is part of the sequence that, tongue-in-cheek, counter-attacked **Al Capp's** "Mary Worm" parody (beginning in this volume August 18, 1957). Artist **Ken Ernst** skillfully caricatures a disheveled and boorish **Capp**. In the second panel writer **Allen Saunders'** dialog pokes fun at **Capp's** only slightly exaggerated "assembly line" of assistants. The specialist doing "ads for that (ugh) cereal!" references the long-running cartoon print ads for **Cream of Wheat** cereal which employed characters from "Li'l Abner." The "hair oil account" refers to the also long-running comic strip ads for **Wildroot Cream Oil**, starring **Fearless Fosdick**.

---

contemporary hit song "Yes Sir, That's My Baby" (last parodied 1/6/57). We meet **Pepe** and **Mimi Yokum**, the Parisian counterparts of **Mammy** and **Pappy**, complete with a fifteen and a half year-old daughter **Babette**, a counterpart to **Tiny**. It should be noted that, while the French were fair game, **Capp** was highly regarded in some French intellectual circles. Filmmaker **Alain Resnais** (*Last Year at Marienbad, Hiroshima Mon Amour*), for one, called **Capp** "America's one immortal myth."

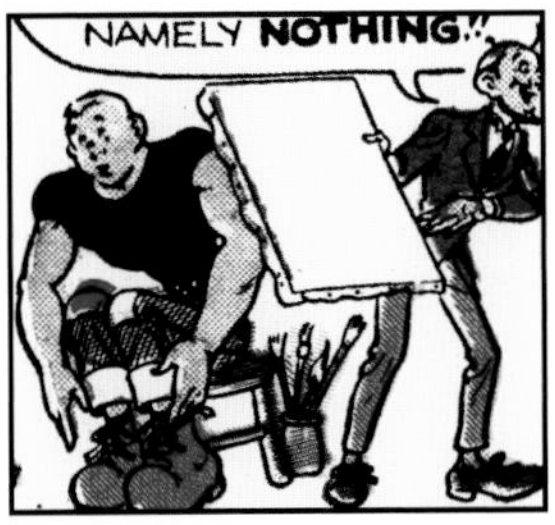
NAMELY NOTHING!!

June 30, 1957. Page 88. **"Kissin' Cousins." (2 of 2). Al Capp's** target here is not the French art scene per se but abstract art in general, a longtime bugaboo. **Tiny Yokum's** prize-winning blank canvas in 1957 was not an original concept and the French judges and the cartoonist both knew it. Russian painter **Kasimir Malevich's** *White on White* (1915) hangs in the Museum of Modern Art. His related *Black Square on White* sold in 2000 for $1 million. American artist **Robert Rauschenberg** created his *White Painting* in 1951, comprising seven monochromatic white panels. **Capp** regarded such notorious works of "art" as intellectual fraud. His oft-quoted observation of abstract art was that it was "the product of the untalented, sold by the unprincipled to the utterly bewildered."

July 7, 1957. Page 89. **"The Senator Investigates P.U." (1 of 3).** The riddle posed in the last panel is no real mystery. Regular readers know with certainty that **Li'l Abner** will be the recipient of the implant next week.

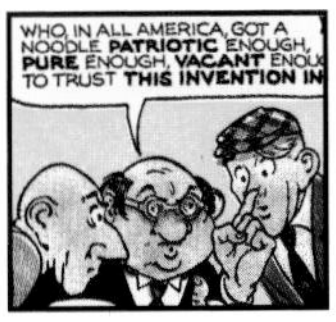
WHO, IN ALL AMERICA, GOT A NOODLE PATRIOTIC ENOUGH, PURE ENOUGH, VACANT ENOUGH TO TRUST THIS INVENTION IN

July 14, 1957. Page 90. **"The Boy Who Knew Too Much!!" (2 of 3).** *The Man Who Knew Too Much* was a **G. K. Chesterton** novel, adapted into a film by **Alfred Hitchcock** the year "Li'l Abner" began.

July 21, 1957. Page 91. **"The Facts of Life!!" (3 of 3).** It's a typical government boondoggle (and a confirmation of **Capp's** own obsession): U.S. taxpayer money goes to employ thousands and spend billions for twenty years, ultimately to learn that people "allus thinks o' th' same ole thing"...*sex*.

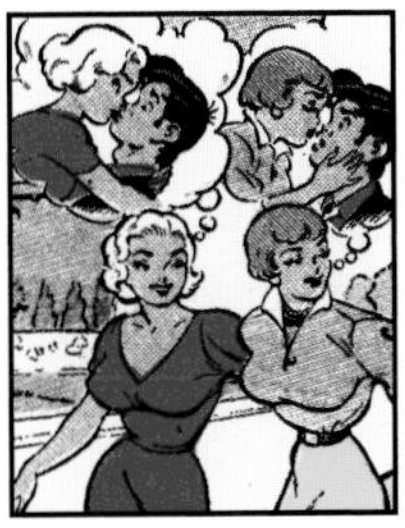

July 28, 1957. Page 92. **"The Snake Slithers Into Eden." (1 of 3).**

August 4, 1957. Page 93. **"Slug Thy Neighbor!" (2 of 3).** Capp, as has probably been noted, has a tendency to repeat strip titles. This one was used as recently as June.

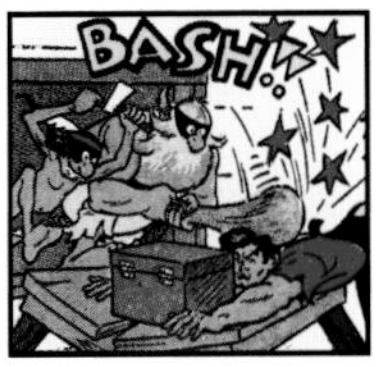
BASH!!

August 11, 1957. Page 94. **"The Best Things in Life are Free!!" (3 of 3).**

August 18, 1957. Page 95. **"The Secret Life of Mary Worm." (1 of 3). Li'l Abner** has long been addicted to the strip-within-a-strip "Fearless Fosdick," a parody of **Chester Gould's** "Dick Tracy." Now we learn that **Daisy Mae** is also hooked on a comic strip. "Mary Worm, America's most beloved old Busybody," is based on "Mary Worth," a character **Al Capp** had taken at least one other potshot at earlier (see the 4/3/55 Sunday). **Capp** made a very good living skewering celebrities, politicians, and the popular culture, including other comics. But *this* time, the worm turned. "Mary Worth" creator and writer **Allen Saunders ("Allen Flounder")** and his collaborator **Ken Ernst** skewered back. In their own daily strip, running concurrently, they featured a boorish, ill-tempered, and egotistical cartoonist named **Hal Rapp**,

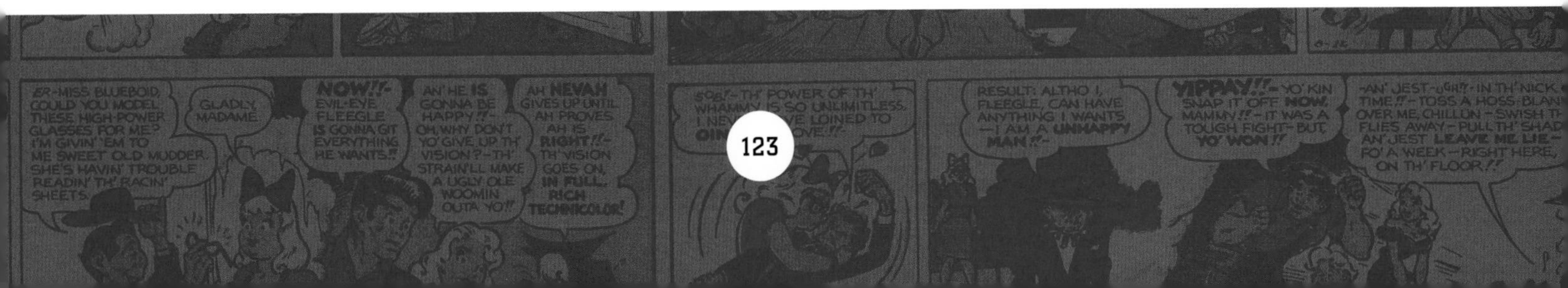

creator of "Big Abe." The national media lavished attention on the feuding cartoonists, quoting **Capp** saying, "Mary Worth is a nasty, black-hearted, nosy old hag," with **Saunders** retorting, "Al Capp is surrounded by phonies—he doesn't know any real, true, honest people." Even *Time* magazine ran an illustrated article on the feud in their "Press" section.

The "feud" was revealed as a hoax. The main clue was that the strips ran concurrently. Factoring syndicate lead time, a genuine feud would have required an offended party's counter-parody to lag by at least six weeks behind the first volley fired. According to **Capp**, he and **Saunders** invented and coordinated the public spat because "we cartoonists decided that ours was the dullest possible profession, since we all liked each other. We decided it might add some interest to the entire profession if a couple of us murdered each other."

In claiming that cartoonists "all like each other" **Capp** failed to mention his long-running, extraordinarily bitter and public feud with "Joe Palooka" creator **Ham Fisher**, a feud that ended only when **Fisher**, foiled in an effort to expose **Capp** as a pornographer, committed suicide in December 1955.

The **Mary Worm/Hal Rapp** "feud" was not the first cross-parody scheme concocted by **Al Capp**. In 1947 he called cartoonist **Will Eisner** and proposed that **Eisner** parody "Li'l Abner" in his syndicated Sunday newspaper insert, "The Spirit," promising to reciprocate in "Li'l Abner." **Eisner**, flattered by the attention of his profession's preeminent figure, quickly complied, creating a "Li'l Adam, the Stupid Mountain Boy" episode (7/20/47). *Newsweek* got wind of the parody in advance (presumably from **Capp**), and ran an article in their 7/21/47 issue, focusing in good part on **Capp**, who never reciprocated with the promised

"Spirit" parody. "I kept watching and waiting and nothing happened," **Eisner** recalled years later. "I then realized that he had euchred me into doing a parody of 'Li'l Abner,' which *Newsweek* picked up, and he had been given a run of publicity. I was simply being used as a tool."

August 25, 1957. Page 96. "Mary Worm Rides Again." (2 of 3).

September 1, 1957. Page 97. "To Each His Own." (3 of 3). The title is taken from the 1946 **Olivia de Havilland** film.

 **September 8, 1957.** Page 98. "The Worm Turns!!" (1 of 4). **Al Capp** exploited his characters for years, so it is only inevitable that his primary two-dimensional employees eventually rebel and seek greener pastures. The first strip that **Li'l Abner** considers moving to is "Snuffy Smith." **Daisy Mae's** dismissive "wouldn't be no change" retort is because "Snuffy" is another hillbilly strip. **Walt Kelly's** "Pogo" is suggested because it's also a southern locale (Okefenoke Swamp is on the Georgia/Florida border). **Harold Gray's** "Li'l Orphan Annie" was parodied by **Capp** in his January 1953 Sundays as "Sweet Fanny Gooney." The name was a combination of "Little Orphan Annie" and a lesser-known strip, "Little Annie Rooney," but the parody was unmistakably aimed at the former (super-patriot **Daddy Warbucks** in the parody becomes **Uncle Sawbuck**, a communist spy who tries to kill the heroine).

September 15, 1957. Page 99. "Take Me Out to the Bald Game." (2 of 4). **Al Capp** quickly jumps from one comic strip parody

to another. But instead of "feuding" with a competing cartoonist, this time he drops **Li'l Abner** into much friendlier turf. As noted in earlier annotations, **Capp** and **Milton Caniff** were the closest of friends, going back to their $50/week jobs at the Associated Press in 1932. **Capp**, a Jew, ribs his gentile friend here by calling him **Milton "Goniff"** (Yiddish for "thief") and changing "Steve Canyon" to "Cantor" (the chanter of liturgical materials in a synagogue). **Capp** had used the "Milton Goniff" pen name before as the author of his 1/53 "Little Orphan Annie" parody." **Capp** and his assistants do a remarkable job of transforming the style of the strip to **Caniff's** distinctive inking style. Even the lettering closely mimics that of "Steve Canyon." The name of bald villain **Jewel Brynner** comes from bald actor **Yul Brynner**, who was caricatured as **Errol Skinn** as recently as April 7th.

September 22, 1957. Page 100. "The Bald and the Beautiful." (3 of 4). *The Bad and the Beautiful* was a 1952 **Kirk Douglas** film.

September 29, 1957. Page 101. "When the Indigestible Meets the Incorruptible!!" (4 of 4).

October 6, 1957. Page 102. "Jayney Get Your Gum." (1 of 1). The title is a play on "Annie Get Your Gun," the Broadway musical. "*This* is a Life?"  is yet another spoof of "This is Your Life" (last parodied March 7 to 21, 1954 when **Mammy Yokum** also appeared on stage). Voluptuous actress **Jayne Cornfield** is based on **Jayne Mansfield**. The TV host's comment that she is Hollywood's "healthiest" new star is **Capp's** code for Hollywood's "most buxom" star. Her name was also parodied in the strip on 5/19/57 as Jayne **Mansfeet**. Screechnut chewing gum is Beechnut.

October 13, 1957. Page 103. "Nightmare Alice in Wonderland!!" (1 of 1). "Witchkraft Theatre" is a play on "Kraft Television Theatre."

October 20, 1957. Page 104. "The Wilkes-Barresaurus." (1 of 2). Why would **Al Capp**, whose wordplay was consistently clever, name a dinosaur a Wilkes-Barresaurus?

There's no logical joke or prehistoric pun associated with the Pennsylvania mining town. The awkward-sounding name can only be understood in the context of **Capp's** life-long enmity against "Joe Palooka" creator **Ham Fisher**, a proud Wilkes-Barre native, who died nearly two years earlier. Other than regarding his late competitor as an "iggorant," ugly, plodding dinosaur

and "an ongrateful varmint," the full meaning of the posthumous barb may only have been known to himself and a few cronies.

October 27, 1957. Page 105. "Bachelor Party." (2 of 2).

November 3, 1957. Page 106. "Hurricane Daisy!!" (1 of 4). **Daisy Mae** has suffered many indignities over the years, from losing her boyfriend/ husband Li'l Abner in countless cruel ways, being abducted, losing her identity, and being subjected to extreme obesity. Being bow-legged for a month, in context, is a minor indignity.

November 10, 1957. Page 107. "From Rags to Ritziness." (2 of 4). The shrewd businessman selling **Abner** a dress at a usurious rate is **Soft-Hearted John**, Dogpatch's only retailer.

November 17, 1957. Page 108. "I Married a Bow-legged Star." (3 of 4). While **Daisy Mae** is temporarily above common work,

and **Li'l Abner** very reluctantly labors to pay off her $350 dress, it should be pointed out that **Pappy Yokum** is truly lazy. He's so lazy he can't even *bathe* himself. **Mammy Yokum** invariably and—by Dogpatch standards—frequently bathes her helpless husband, as in this episode. Modesty is not an issue: often the wooden bathtub is outdoors.

November 24, 1957. Page 109. "Scrambled Legs!!" (4 of 4). **Randolph Squat** spoofs western actor **Randolph Scott**.

December 1, 1957. Page 110. "Go Home Joe Btfsplk!!" (1 of 5). One of **Al Capp's** most enduring and memorable characters is **Joe Btfsplk**, a fixture in the strip since 1942. The sad little man with a wide brim hat, an unpronounceable name, and a perpetual rain cloud over his head, is the world's worst jinx. The **Adlai** he "helped" is

Joe Btfsplk button drawn by Frank Frazetta.

Stevenson, the losing Democratic Party nominee for president in 1956. **Sugar Ray Robinson** was the middleweight boxing champion until he lost the crown to **Carmen Basilio** in a controversial split decision in September 1957. **Joe** also "helped" ambitious Soviet Union Premier **Georgi Malenkov** in his effort to oust leader **Nikita Khrushchev** in June 1957. **Khrushchev** prevailed and **Malenkov** was exiled to a remote corner of Siberia. But **Btfsplk** is free, and doom for someone is certain to follow.

December 8, 1957. Page 111. "The Voice of the Turtle Dove." (2 of 5). Dogpatch, the downtrodden jinx's own hometown, actually has a warning bell that sounds

when he approaches. **Li'l Abner**, his "only friend in th' world," turns **Joe** back at the point of a rifle. But **Al Capp** himself didn't recoil in fear. When he retired in 1977, a reporter asked him which of his many

characters he was most fond of. He cited **Mammy Yokum** and…**Joe Btfsplk**. And, for the record, according to **Capp**, **Btfsplk's** last name is not unpronounceable. When spoken it resembles the spittle-flying, tongue-between-lips sound one makes when "giving someone the raspberries," also known as a "Bronx cheer."

December 15, 1957. Page 112. "When Greek Meets Greek." (3 of 5). The title comes from the proverb, "When Greek meets Greek, then comes the tug-of-war,"

referring to a contest in which each side has equal strength.

December 22, 1957. Page 113. "Love Finds a Way." (4 of 5).

December 29, 1957. Page 114. "Ah, Sweet Misery of Life." (5 of 5). The title comes from "Ah, Sweet Mystery of Life," a decades-old song popularized by both **Nelson Eddy** and **Mario Lanza**  which **Capp** has used before. Telephone operator **Dawn Ameche's** name comes from actor **Don Ameche**, whose film portrayal of **Alexander Graham Bell** made him long synonymous with telephones. The best known talking horse, **Mister Ed**, did not hit the small screen till 1961. The talking mule reference here is to an earlier, lesser known, but equally loquacious equine, **Francis the Talking Mule**, who starred in a half dozen B-movies between 1949 and 1955.

The next story, encompassing six episodes, will run in Volume 3.

HERE COMES A DOUBLE WHAMMY FROM YOUR FAVORITE COMICAL STRIP

Li'l ABNER®

Al Capp

Li'L ABNER®
THE FRAZETTA YEARS

Edited and Commentary by Denis Kitchen
VOLUME 1 1954-1955

AL CAPP'S LI'L ABNER:
THE FRAZETTA YEARS VOLUME 1
ISBN: 1-56971-959-4 $18.95

LIMITED EDITION LI'L ABNER
CLASSIC COMIC CHARACTERS STATUES

Modeled after vintage "syroco" statues that featured characters from the comic strips of the 1930s–'40s. Each numbered statue comes packaged in a full-color tin box and includes a vintage-style pin-back button of the character.

$49.95 each

LI'L ABNER
Item #19-390

DAISY MAE
Item #19-403

FEARLESS FOSDICK
Item #19-550

SHMOO
Item #10-334

ALSO AVAILABLE FROM DARK HORSE COMICS:

COMICS BETWEEN THE PANELS

by Steve Duin and Mike Richardson

This lavish, full-color, coffee-table style hardcover celebrates the comics medium by taking an idiosyncratic look at everything from creators, characters, and companies to conventions and collectors. Richardson and Duin provide the inside scoop on the early days of comics in the 1930s, the studio days of the 1940s, the crisis of the 1950s, and the resurgence in the 1960s. A must-have for anyone fascinated by comics and the rich history of the medium.
500pg/hardcover/9" x 12"/Ages 10+

ISBN: 1-56971-344-8 $49.95

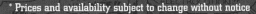